THE INTERNET:
A TOOL FOR
CAREER PLANNING

THIRD EDITION

DEBRA S. OSBORN

MARGARET RILEY DIKEL

JAMES P. SAMPSON, JR.

FOREWORD BY
JOANN HARRIS-BOWLSBEY

National Career Development Association

A founding division of the American Counseling Association

© Copyright 2011 by the National Career Development Association
305 North Beech Circle
Broken Arrow, OK 74012
Phone: (918) 663-7060
Fax: (918) 663-7058

NCDA opposes discrimination against any individual based on age, culture, disability, ethnicity, race, religion/spirituality, creed, gender, gender identity and expression, sexual orientation, marital/partnership status, language preference, socioeconomic status, any other characteristics not specifically relevant to job performance.

NCDA Board of Directors, March 2010

Library of Congress Cataloging-in-Publication Data

Osborn, Debra S., 1968-
The internet : a tool for career planning / Debra S. Osborn, Margaret F.
Dikel, James P. Sampson, Jr. ; foreword by JoAnn Harris-Bowlsbey. -- 3rd ed.
        p. cm.
ISBN 978-1-885333-30-8
1. Vocational guidance--Computer network resources. 2. Career
development--Computer network resources. 3. Internet. 4. World Wide Web.
I. Dikel, Margaret F. II. Sampson, James P. III. Title.
HF5382.7.H367 2011
650.10285'4678--dc22
                    2011007687

ABOUT THE AUTHORS

Debra S. Osborn is an associate professor of counselor education in the Department of Psychological & Social Foundations at the University of South Florida. Her research has focused on career development in youth and young adults; career development issues with high risk youth; use of technology in training; increasing competency and confidence in counseling students; and career satisfaction of counselors.

Margaret Riley Dikel is the author of The Riley Guide (rileyguide.com) and co-author of *The Guide to Internet Job Searching*. Margaret is a recognized expert in the online job-and-career industry, beginning her review of the many sites and services available in 1994. She is a private consultant working with the organizations who aid job seekers, and she holds a Master of Science in Library and Information Sciences from Simmons College.

James P. Sampson, Jr., is the Mode L. Stone Distinguished Professor of Counseling and Career Development in the Department of Educational Psychology and Learning Systems at Florida State University. Along with Robert C. Reardon, he established the Center for the Study of Technology in Counseling and Career Development, a research center dedicated to improving the design and use of computer applications in counseling and guidance.

FOREWORD

By JoAnn Harris-Bowlsbey

The whole incredible idea of using technology to assist young people and adults with career development and planning began in the mid-1960s occasioned by the introduction of a computer monitor by IBM. This device, with the capability of being placed as much as 1,000 feet away from a mainframe, made it possible for someone who had created a structured dialogue and programmed it into the computer to communicate with a student or adult who worked from the terminal device in an interactive mode. Early developers like Donald E. Super, David V. Tiedeman, Martin R. Katz, and myself recognized the potential of simulating counselor interviews, administering and interpreting assessments, teaching and monitoring career development skills (such as decision making), displaying information, and searching large databases by multiple characteristics. Along with all of these capabilities, we also recognized the capability to store a unique user record (now often called an electronic portfolio) for each student or client which could be a repository for ongoing career choices and documents, such as resumes or certifications, that are relevant to career progression.

The early developers struggled to harness the technology to fulfill their dreams of how it could be used to support the career development of individuals of all ages. Super and Tiedeman tried to make the technology display pictures and graphics long before it was capable of doing so. Tiedeman tried to make the technology capable of word recognition decades before it was capable of doing so. Katz and Tiedeman were passionate about using the technology to teach system users a process which they would then internalize and use again and again. Harris-Bowlsbey tried to make the technology capable of searching the characteristics of thousands of college/university descriptions and producing a list of qualified options, all within 48K of RAM. In these first attempts, there were many failures and many amazing discoveries about the power and limitations of this new tool.

Forty years later, all of the dreams of the early developers are easily attainable. In fact, the technology is moving forward so quickly that today's developers can hardly keep up with ways to harness and use the power of current computers. Counselors no longer believe that developers are trying to replace them, but rather accept technology as an ordinary valuable tool that assists them to do their work daily. Research continues to support the early findings that technology alone can provide some very positive benefits for its users, but that additional benefits are provided when the technology is supported by a knowledgeable human. High touch and high tech have become collaborative and cozy bedfellows.

The authors of this book are today's leaders in the field of web-enabled career information and counseling. In their respective chapters they share the very latest with you. Your reading of this book will bring you up to date, and perhaps hold you there for at least six months! What does the future of technology in our field hold? Will its capabilities combined with the human communication now possible through it offer a new, more cost-feasible, and higher level of career planning and placement service for individuals worldwide than we have ever known?

PREFACE

Technology and the Internet are among the career practitioner's most vital tools in helping individuals make career decisions. Since its first edition, the purpose of this book has been to provide career practitioners with information about how to use online resources to enhance the career decision-making process. The aim was to provide more than a list and description of important websites, although that was one intent. Even more important was the discussion about issues involved in using Internet resources in career service delivery, both with face-to-face clients and as an online presence accessible by everyone.

This book is the third edition of *The Internet: A Tool for Career Planning.* While the initial goals for this book have remained the same, the technologies have changed, and the issues surrounding the use of the Internet in career service provision have become more complex. In the second edition, social networking sites (SNSs) were just beginning to emerge. Today, membership and communication through these SNSs is becoming a preferred mode of connecting and communicating, and thus have become useful tools in the job search. At the time of the previous edition, most career centers had an online presence, but today we are seeing career centers and career practitioners providing real-time services online, and some career websites provide services completely online. Thus, we have included a discussion on how to create a virtual career center.

Other advances in career development research have impacted the writing of this third edition. For example, client readiness to use career services is a new topic in this edition. While readiness research has focused primarily on clients seeking face-to-face career services and their readiness to engage in the career decision-making process, there are similar implications for clients wanting to engage in that process online. Finally, there are also new ethical dilemmas emerging as the Internet becomes a more important part of clients' and career practitioners' lives. In the previous edition, the main ethical concerns were about the validity, reliability, and security of online career testing, as well as the relevancy, currency, and accuracy of career websites. Because of technology changes, this edition adds to the original ethical issues that are still of concern and addresses the ethics involved in the use of distance counseling and social networking sites related to the career planning process.

After providing some background information on the use of information in career planning and decision making in Chapter 1, the use of information and interaction among counselors and clients is presented in Chapters 2, 3, and 4. A comprehensive description of online career resources is presented in Chapter 5. Ethical issues that relate to information and interactions among counselors and clients are presented in Chapter 6. While this book represents a collaborative work of the authors, each chapter had a primary writer. Osborn was the primary author for Chapters 1 and 4; Sampson was the primary author for Chapters 2, 3, and 6; Dikel was the primary author for Chapter 5; and Harris-Bowlsbey contributed to each chapter.

The conceptual scheme for the chapters is shown below.

CHAPTER 1			
Information and Career Decision Making			
CHAPTER 2 Use of the Internet in Face-to-Face and Distance Counseling	**CHAPTER 3** Use of the Internet in Virtual Career Centers	**CHAPTER 4** Use of Social Networking in Delivering Career Services	**CHAPTER 5** Online Resources for Career Decision Making
CHAPTER 6			
Potential Ethical Problems			

The coordinating author expresses her thanks to Margaret Riley Dikel, James P. Sampson, Jr., and JoAnn Harris-Bowlsbey for their dedicated, tireless efforts in pursuing excellence with respect to the information in this book. The authors also wish to thank Deneen Pennington and Mary Ann Powell at NCDA Headquarters, and Robert Reardon who provided guidance and unwavering support for this project. It is our hope that this book will serve as a useful tool for career practitioners who are seeking to use the Internet and its vast resources to enhance the career decision-making process for their clients.

TABLE OF CONTENTS

CHAPTER 1
INFORMATION AND
CAREER DECISION MAKING

The purpose of this book is to explore the wealth of career information and assessment tools available on the Internet and to provide suggestions on how career practitioners can use this information successfully with their students and clients. In our opinion, the foundation for effectively using the Internet to enhance career planning and career decision-making requires two elements: (a) an ability of the client and career practitioner to communicate with each other, and (b) the ability to easily access information from career websites.

In this chapter, we review how information is used in different career decision-making theories and models, identify types and sources of information, and explore ways to evaluate information. We then turn our attention to the benefits and challenges of using online resources with clients and students, and present a model for doing so. Given that information that is current, relevant, and of high quality is essential to the process of career decision making, it seems appropriate to begin this chapter with a definition of the term "information."

Defining Information

Before we begin, it might be useful to provide some definitions, directly quoted from http://merriam-webster.com/dictionary:

- **Information:** the communication or reception of knowledge or intelligence
- **Knowledge:** the fact or condition of knowing something with familiarity gained through experience or association
- **Fact:** the quality of being actual; something that has actual existence
- **Data:** factual information used as the basis for reasoning, discussion, or calculation
- **Opinion:** a view, judgment, or appraisal formed in the mind about a particular matter

In reviewing information, it is important to recognize the distinction between fact, data, and opinion. Sometimes opinion is presented as fact. Sometimes, the information is repeated so often that it is assumed to be fact. Facts taken out of one context may not be valid in another. For example, salary information about a position in one region may be significantly higher or lower in a different region. As we will discuss further in the sections below, clients and career practitioners must take care to evaluate information as for its validity and relevance.

What is the Relationship Between Information and Decision Making?

Informed decision making implies a decision that is based on current, valid information from a variety of sources. Information literacy has been defined on the American Library Association's website (American Library Association, 1989) as a set of abilities requiring individuals to "recognize when information is needed and have the ability to locate, evaluate, and use effectively the needed information" (Information Literacy Defined Section, para. 4). Later, the American Library Association (2000) wrote the *Information Literacy Competency Standards for Higher Education*, describing on their website that an information literate individual is able to

- determine the extent of information needed,
- access the needed information effectively and efficiently,
- evaluate information and its sources critically,
- incorporate selected information into one's knowledge base,
- use information effectively to accomplish a specific purpose,
- understand the economic, legal, and social issues surrounding the use of information, and
- access and use information ethically and legally (Information Literacy Defined Section, para. 6).

How Do We Know When Students/Clients Are Ready to Make Effective Use of Information?

Readiness for career decision making involves the "capability" of individuals to solve problems given the "complexity" of their life circumstances (Sampson, 2008). Capability refers to internal factors that make it more, or less, difficult for individuals to decide about occupational, educational, training, or employment options.

Elements of capability include:

- Honesty in exploring interests, skills, and values
- Motivation to learn about occupational, educational, training, and employment options
- Capacity to think clearly about a career problem
- Confidence in being able to make a good choice
- Willingness to accept personal responsibility for career decision making
- Awareness of how negative thoughts and feelings potentially limit decision making
- Willingness to seek assistance with a career choice when needed
- Awareness of progress through decision making, for example, awareness of when adequate information exists to make a choice

Complexity refers to external factors that make it more, or less, difficult to decide about occupational, educational, training, or employment options. Specific aspects of complexity include the family, society, the economy, and organizations (for persons who are employed). A variety of circumstances have a positive and negative influence on problem solving, making it easier or more difficult. Four aspects of complexity that reduce readiness for problem solving are described in Figure 1.1.

A client's readiness directly impacts the level of practitioner support needed. Specifically, someone with low readiness would need more regular, intensive support; someone with moderate readiness would require less but still some brief support; while someone with high readiness would require little to no support or could be self-directed. A two-dimensional model showing the interaction between capability and complexity is presented below in Figure 1.2.

Figure 1.1 Aspects of Complexity

FAMILY
- Multiple family responsibilties or stressors
- Deferral (compromising one's career development for needs of family members)
- Role overload (difficulty balancing one's work with homemaking and childcare)
- Dysfunctional family input
- Unsupportive family members
- Health problems of a family member

SOCIETY
- Poor social support (inadequate role models, poor mentoring, and limited networking)
- Stereotyping
- Discrimination
- Harrassment

ECONOMY
- Inadequate personal finances for education and job relocation
- Unstable labor market due to rapid economic change

EMPLOYING ORGANIZA-TIONS
- (For persons who are employed)
- Large organizations with more complicated internal job markets
- Lack of employer support for employee career development
- Unstable organizations with less predictable employment opportunities

Individuals who have a high level of decision-making capability and a low level of life complexity generally have a higher level of readiness and experience less difficulty in making choices. These persons are more likely to make successful use of the resources described in Chapter 5 on a self-help basis or with brief assistance from a practitioner. Individuals who have a low level of decision-making capability and a high level of life complexity generally have a lower level of readiness and experience more difficulty in making choices. These persons are less likely to make successful use of web-based career resources and will need more individualized assistance from a practitioner over time. In addition to capability and complexity, a variety of other constructs can be used to assess readiness for problem solving (Sampson, Peterson, Reardon, & Lenz, 2000).

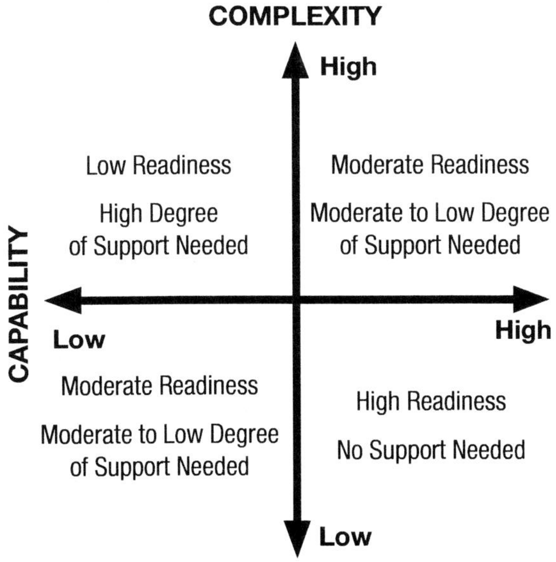

It is important for practitioners to recognize characteristics of high and low readiness in order to determine the level of support necessary (Sampson, Reardon, Peterson, & Lenz, 2004). Table 1.1 presents these differences.

Figure 1.2 Model of Client Readiness

COMPLEXITY

High

| Low Readiness | Moderate Readiness |
| High Degree of Support Needed | Moderate to Low Degree of Support Needed |

Low ← → High

CAPABILITY

| Moderate Readiness | High Readiness |
| Moderate to Low Degree of Support Needed | No Support Needed |

Low

Table 1.1 Characteristics of High and Low Readiness

HIGH READINESS	LOW READINESS
• Fewer family, social, economic, and organizational factors to cope with in career problem solving and decision making • Honesty in self-exploration • Appropriate verbal aptitude • Appropriate literacy in English • Appropriate reading ability • Absence of a significant learning disability (Sampson, 2004)	• Poor motivation to engage in problem solving • Inability to think clearly • Lack of confidence in decision-making ability • Lack of commitment to carry out a plan of action • Unwillingness to accept responsibility for problem solving • Limited understanding of the problem-solving process

Clients with low readiness for problem solving will need more careful orientation to the websites. More effective orientation for persons with low readiness may reduce the anxiety associated with using a website, leading to more complete and more effective use of a site. Also, clients with low readiness for problem solving may benefit from a career practitioner modeling information-seeking behavior by briefly demonstrating a pathway for moving through the site to obtain an assessment, an information resource, or an opportunity for personal communication. It is important, however, to avoid overwhelming the client with more orientation information than the client can understand and use at one time. Clients with high readiness may need only minimal orientation to the website, in some cases relying principally on the orientation and help features included on the site.

How Do Career Decision-Making Models Use Information?

Elements of informed career decision making have been suggested by career theorists and researchers (Parsons, 1909; Sampson et al., 2004; Shahnasarian, 2005). Parsons based his approach to career development on the interface between a person's self-understanding and "conditions of success" for particular jobs. Specifically, Parsons believed that certain elements were necessary for effective decision-making. Table 1-2 outlines these specifics.

Other career theorists have added to Parsons' list by elaborating on the types of self and occupational information needed to make informed career decisions. For example, cognitive information processing theory (Sampson et al., 2004) lists values, interests, skills, and employment preferences as necessary self-knowledge components for career decision making, and knowledge of individual occupations and a schema for organizing the world of work as necessary for occupational knowledge. In addition to several of the variables listed above, Donald Super (1980) suggested that needs, intelligence, achievement, and specific aptitudes should also be considered for an understanding of self, and the economy, education, labor markets, and employment practices for an understanding of occupations. In his identification and description of six types of vocational interests, John Holland (1997) also added personality to the mix of elements required for self-knowledge.

Table 1.2 Elements Necessary for an Effective Decision

SELF-UNDERSTANDING	REQUIREMENTS AND CONDITIONS OF SUCCESS
Ancestry Family Education Reading Experience Interests Aptitudes Abilities Ambitions Preparation Resources Limitations and their causes	Initial requirements Advantages and disadvantages Compensations Opportunities Prospects Means of preparation development . . . in different lines of work

The National Career Development Association (NCDA) has identified knowledge of and skills in "Information/Resources" as one of several career counseling competencies required for effective career practitioners. Specifically, NCDA (National Career Development Association, 1997, see Information/Resources, p. 5) outlines the following minimum standards for knowledge and skills:

1. Education, training, and employment trends; labor market information and resources that provide information about job tasks, functions, salaries, requirements, and future outlooks related to broad occupational fields and individual occupations.

2. Resources and skills that clients utilize in life-work planning and management.

3. Community/professional resources available to assist clients in career planning, including job search.

4. Changing roles of women and men and the implications that this has for education, family, and leisure.

5. Methods of good use of computer-based career information delivery systems (CIDS) and computer-assisted career guidance systems (CACGS) to assist with career planning.

In reviewing these recommended areas for investigation, we can see that individuals have an extensive need for specific types of information about themselves and another type of information about occupations.

What Are the Types of Information Individuals Need?

Various types of information exist for self-knowledge and knowledge about occupations/options and the world of work. For building self-knowledge, possible types of information include standardized and nonstandardized career assessments, and reflective experiences such as autobiographies and responses to open-ended questions.

Information about options may be presented in many different forms, such as:

- Books, articles, magazines, newspapers
- Professional career information sites, such as O*NET and the Occupational Outlook Handbook (U. S. Department of Labor, Bureau of Labor Statistics, 2010–2011)
- Experiential activities such as volunteering, internships, and work
- Third-party accounts (a friend of a friend knows someone in that field)

- Job descriptions
- Social networking sites
- Podcasts
- Interviews

- Websites
- Wikipedia or other encyclopedia entries
- Blogs
- Television, radio

The Internet exponentially increases the volume of such types of information. However, users may not be information literate or able to distinguish between valid, useful information and information that is invalid or biased.

What Are the Sources of Information About Options?

Two common sources for web-based career information include the online *Occupational Outlook Handbook* (http://www.bls.gov/oco/), and the O*NET. The *Occupational Outlook Handbook* was developed by the U.S. Bureau of Labor Statistics and is revised every two years. It provides information on significant points about occupations including the nature of the work; training, other qualifications, and advancement; information on employment; job outlook; earnings; related occupations; and sources for additional information. In addition, the site is beginning to include occupational information in Spanish.

The O*NET (http://online.onetcenter.org) was created by the National Center for O*NET Development. Within this site, users can browse through groups of related organizations to explore career possibilities, research specific occupations, identify career options that meet specific skills, or use a crosswalk between sources such as the *Occupational Outlook Handbook*, Standard Occupational Classification System (SOC numbers), or Military Careers. Information can be provided in a summary or detailed format. Specific details include tasks, tools and technology, knowledge, skills, abilities, work activities, work content, job zone, education, interests, work styles, work values, related occupations, wages and employment, and additional information.

Chapter 5 provides a detailed list of online resources that might be used to provide actual sources for the types of information listed above. The information in Chapter 5 is organized under the following headings:

- Apprenticeships and other alternative training programs
- Career development process
- Career search engines
- Directories of online employment and career guides.
- Employment trends
- Educational information
- Financial aid information
- Job banks

- Job search instruction and advice
- Occupational information
- Resources and services for ex-offenders
- Resources and services for youth, teens, and young adults
- Research employers
- Resources for diverse audiences

- Resources for people with disabilities
- Resources for specific industries and occupations
- Resources for the older client
- Resources to aid separating military personnel and veterans' spouses
- Salary information
- Self-assessment

How Can Career Professionals and Consumers Evaluate Available Information?

With the plethora of information available on the Internet, one of the responsibilities for career development practitioners is to help clients locate and evaluate information. NCDA has provided several checklists to help practitioners evaluate occupational information provided in career software, career and occupational information literature, and video career media (http://associationdatabase.com/aws/NCDA/pt/sp/guidelines). In addition, in their *Consumer Guide for Evaluating Career Information and Services* (Association of Computer-Based Systems for Career Information, 2007, pp. 3–5), the Association of Computer-Based Systems for Career Information (ACSCI) described standards in seven areas, including:

- **Career information:** Career information comprises educational, occupational, industry, financial aid, job search, and related information for career development. Career information should be accurate, current, developmentally appropriate, relevant, specific, unbiased, understandable, and valid for intended audiences.

- **Occupational information:** Occupational information includes the basic characteristics of work being performed by individuals who hold jobs having similar duties, levels of responsibility, skills, knowledge, entry requirements, and physical demands.

- **Industry information:** Industry information includes characteristics of the labor market and economic conditions affecting employers who produce similar products or provide similar services.

- **Education and training information:** Education/training information includes postsecondary educational programs and the schools or other providers offering them, including public and private colleges, universities, career schools, technical schools, and trade associations.

- **Financial aid information:** Financial aid includes information about sources of college student financial aid, procedures for applying for aid, and the criteria for awarding such aid. Financial aid awards include grants, scholarships, loans, and employment. Currency is of the utmost importance in presenting financial aid information.

- **Job search information:** Job search information includes information about what employers seek in prospective employees, job vacancy listings, techniques for obtaining employment, and methods of documenting preparation, experience, and references.

Given the large number of factors that practitioners and clients must consider when using Internet sites, having some type of thorough checklist can be useful. Osborn (2008) created an evaluation worksheet aimed at combining the information from NCDA and ACSCI (http://www.debosborn.com/teaching_examples/Career_Website_Evaluation.pdf) as an attempt to provide a comprehensive list. Even if a checklist is not completed, a career practitioner should spend some time reviewing any website that she or he is considering using with a client, keeping in mind the criteria outlined above.

What Are the Benefits of Using Web-Based Resources with Students/Clients?

Career practitioners have the option of giving clients information or referring clients to valid information from carefully selected websites on the Internet. There are several potential benefits associated with providing information to clients via the Internet:

- The career information provided on a website may be more current and more complete than the information provided by a practitioner. This, of course, assumes that the career information provided on the website is valid, which is not always the case.

- Obtaining career information from a website may lessen the client expectation that the practitioner's role is to provide expert information after the client carefully explains his or her problem, i.e., "Now that I have told you my problem, what do I do?"

- Some clients react negatively to information provided by a practitioner and engage in "Yes, but ..." interactions. Emphasizing a *collaborative* role where the practitioner focuses on helping the client *find* and effectively use information, rather than emphasizing an *authoritarian* role where the practitioner focuses on providing information, may reduce the likelihood of the client responding negatively to the perceived "advice" given by an authority figure.

- Making greater use of online career information may help the practitioner become less focused on being knowledgeable about an ever increasing amount of information related to making career, educational, training, and employment decisions. Again, the role of the practitioner shifts from *providing* information to helping clients *find* and effectively use the information they need, i.e., the practitioner's role is less about the *content* of decision making and more about the *process* of decision making. Helping clients better understand why they are reluctant to use the information they have obtained is a "higher order" provider function than that of giving information.

- Obtaining online information may help clients assume more responsibility for decision making since they are not dependent on the practitioner for getting access to information.

- Helping the client learn how to obtain and effectively use information may empower the client to be a better problem solver in the future.

The role of the practitioner will always include the provision of information, such as information that is so specific or localized that it is not available on the Internet. The task of the practitioner is to make good judgments about when to provide information directly to the client and when to recommend that the client obtain information from a specific portion of a website. The ultimate aim is to help clients obtain and use good quality information that they can effectively use in solving problems and making decisions.

What Are the Challenges of Using Web-Based Resources with Students/Clients?

Career practitioners must acknowledge that certain challenges exist in using online resources with students and clients, and practitioners should evaluate the potential impact of each of these challenges for each individual.

- Every client varies in their access to online resources; this has an impact on the amount of support a career practitioner provides. For example, clients that are very competent and confident may only need to be provided with links that they can access outside of a session, whereas clients who are low on both areas might require the practitioner to use the resource in the session.

- Not all web-based resources are of equal value. Clients may come in having read about a career or taken an assessment online, but may not have evaluated the validity of the source.

- Availability and accessibility to the Internet will vary. Not all clients will have access to web-based resources. While public locations such as the library may provide Internet access, these sites are not as secure as private locations, which may affect usability.

- Readiness of the client to use web-based resources is another area of concern that should be assessed and not assumed. It is possible that the complexity of the Internet may be challenging for individuals who are already overwhelmed with the process of making a choice.

- Other ethical concerns with respect to online service delivery are discussed in detail in Chapter 6.

What Are Effective Collaborative Models of Using Web-Based Resources in Career Counseling and Guidance?

Three ways that the Internet can be used by career development practitioners to assist students and clients with career decision making include:

1. Upon assessing the needs of an individual, career practitioners can assign specific websites for review.

    a. In order to do this effectively, the practitioner needs to know where the individual is in the decision-making cycle and have a thorough knowledge of the content of specific sites related to common client concerns. This makes it easier for the practitioner to recommend specific and manageable portions of a website that address a specific need of the client.

    b. Further, since content-rich sites may be very comprehensive, it is highly desirable that the practitioner assign specific parts of the site so that the client or student will not be overwhelmed with information.

    c. Ideally, this process would entail the intermittent steps of making a specific assignment, having a group or individual counseling session in which the site content is discussed, assigning additional sites or activities if needed, discussing these, etc.

    d. When the specific information needs of a client cannot be met with websites the practitioner typically uses, the practitioner should model good information seeking behavior during the counseling session to locate valid sources of information that have the potential to meet the client's needs.

2. Distance counseling is a second method of using the Internet, which is described more fully in Chapter 3.

    a. In this method, a practitioner uses the Internet as a means of delivery of career interventions.

    b. This may entail communication between the two parties only or may also include the assignment of specific websites as an information base for counseling.

    c. Chapter 4 discusses the conditions and ethics that should surround this method of career intervention.

3. These two modes of service may be combined to form a virtual career center, an online space that provides an integrated system of websites as well as support of their use by a career professional who is available online.

    a. While the first approach offers a variety of disjointed websites, with integration dependent upon the ability of the client and/or practitioner to make it coherent, this third approach offers a system of connected services from one site.

b. In order to create this mode, the site developer must first design an integrated package of content that can support the career decision-making process and then assemble it by making linkages to existing sites, developing new material, or using a combination of both.

c. Such a site would include all of the component pieces mentioned earlier in this chapter, e.g., assessment, occupational information, educational information, and job-seeking information. In the virtual career center approach, informed and careful decision making may be facilitated by an online career development practitioner who can have video-based, synchronous interviews with clients or students, as well as monitor the use of the assessments and databases.

Client Use of Internet Websites as an Information Resource

To avoid being overwhelmed with the information available on the Internet, a practical approach is to use a model that limits the scope of information by linking website use with specific client goals. A client can make more effective use of a website when a practitioner clarifies the client goals that might be achieved by using specific portions of a site. The following model describes generic client goals for using a website as part of a homework assignment in counseling. Achieving these goals can result in specific counseling outcomes that are also described below.

A Model for Linking Client Goals in Counseling with the Use of Internet

There are three main client goals that can be at least partially achieved from using an Internet website (Sampson, Shy, & Cooley, 2007), including:

1. Help the client to **understand** the nature of his or her problem.
2. Assist the client to **act** in ways that help to solve his or her problem.
3. Help the client to better **cope** with problems that cannot be completely solved.

The following case will be used to illustrate an application of this three-part model.

A 50 year-old adult has become unemployed as a result of his company being acquired by another larger business. He had worked for this company for 24 years in two positions. It has been 18 years since his first and only promotion. He is concerned that he is too old to find another job and that his skills are out of date. He is angry about losing his job after working so hard over such a long period of time to contribute to the success of the company. Due to family circumstances, he is unwilling to leave the small town where he resides. Jobs in the local area generally pay a lower salary in comparison with his previous position in a manufacturing company. He is very anxious about meeting his financial needs. Outplacement counseling is offered to him as a benefit given his long service to the company.

The client and the practitioner agree that the client will use specific portions of a website on unemployment and job search strategies to meet the goals of understanding, acting, and coping described earlier. Each of these three generic goals is described in Table 1.3 along with examples of potential client outcomes.

The use of specific portions of a website is guided by client goals that have been collaboratively established by the client and the practitioner. Since client goals differ, client use of websites differs as well. One client may only use web-based information to promote understanding,

Table 1.3 An Example of Linking Goals with Internet Use

	Goal 1: Understanding	Goal 2: Acting	Goal 3: Coping
Description	Help the client *understand* the nature of the problem.	Assist the client to *act* in ways that help to solve the problem.	Help the client to *cope* with problems that cannot be completely solved
Sample Homework Assignment: Review a portion of a website that . . .	. . . explains what many individuals experience when they have a specific problem.	. . . provides descriptions of specific counseling interventions.	. . . provides personal statements of individuals who have experienced, and coped with, similar problems. A practitioner can also recommend that the client participate in a virtual support group by reading and posting messages on a limited access bulletin board related to the client's problem
Goal of Activity	Client will understand the nature of unemployment and how unemployment can impact an individual.	Client will make an informed decision about the intervention that will best address her or his problem.	Client will learn coping skills that are available and how others have successfully coped with a similar situation.
Potential Client Outcomes	*Describe:* • frequency and causes of unemployment • closings/mergers • others' strategies & success stories • normalize situation • coping strategies • casual factors of employment • see the impact of cognitive distortions • create shared vocabulary • facilitate communication	*Demonstrate:* • decision making skills in choosing an intervention, based on client research of unemployment • evaluation of various intervention options through a pro/con analysis • knowledge of costs for different career services • more realistic expectations for change • less anxiety about receiving services • improved self-esteem (by playing an active role in intervention decisions)	*Experience:* • reduced dysfunctional thinking • cognitive restructuring skills • relaxation techniques for anxiety that may interfere with performance in job interviews • explore alternatives to barriers and identify opportunities • how to monitor anxiety and procrastination as indicator of fear or failure • identify community resources and additional supports • hope for the future

while a second client may use portions of a site to promote both understanding and acting. A third client may only use web-based information for coping. The practitioner and client decide if one, two, or all three goals in this model are appropriate and relevant for the decision at hand.

The three client goals included in this model can be viewed as being ordered in a sequence of steps where the client needs to (a) understand the problem, (b) act to solve the problem, and (c) cope with any aspects of the problem that cannot yet be solved. The assumption is that the client needs to understand his or her situation to help ensure that the course of action taken is appropriate for the problem. A second assumption is that knowing the relative success of the actions taken by the client to solve his or her problem can help to focus coping efforts. While new solutions to old problems are always evolving, the reality is that some problems cannot be solved or can only be partially solved, and some coping efforts are required at least temporarily.

The three client goals presented in this section are described in relation to web-based information. However, the generic nature of these goals means that they apply equally well to other sources of information such as print, audio, or video resources, as well as face-to-face interaction with other individuals.

Summary

Information is a foundational element in career decision making. Career development practitioners must have a basic understanding of what kinds of information are needed by a client to make effective career decisions, and how to navigate through the immense amount of information that the Internet provides. In addition, career practitioners must evaluate online career assessments and information, and teach their clients to do the same. The benefits of using online resources in career counseling were described, and a model for linking client goals with Internet usage was presented. This chapter demonstrates how current, valid information can be used to support the career decision-making process.

References

American Library Association. (1989). *Presidential committee on information literacy. Final report.* Chicago: Author. Retrieved from http://www.ala.org/ala/mgrps/divs/acrl/publications/whitepapers/presidential.cfm

American Library Association (2000). *Information literacy competency standards for higher education.* Chicago: Author. Retrieved from http://www.ala.org/ala/mgrps/divs/acrl/standards/informationliteracycompetency.cfm

Association for Computer-Based Systems for Career Information (2007). *Consumer guide for evaluating career information and services.* Broken Arrow, OK: Author.

Holland, J. L. (1997). *Making vocational choices: A theory of vocational personalities and work environments.* Odessa, FL: Psychological Assessment Resources.

National Career Development Association. (1997). http://associationdatabase.com/aws/NCDA/asset_manager/get_file/3397 Information/Resources. Author.

Osborn, D. S. (2008). *Teaching career development: A primer for presenters and instructors.* Broken Arrow, OK: National Career Development Association.

Parsons, F. (2005, reprint). *Choosing a vocation.* Broken Arrow, OK: National Career Development Association.

Sampson, J. P., Jr. (2008). *Designing and implementing career programs: A handbook for effective practice.* Broken Arrow, OK: National Career Development Association.

Sampson, J. P., Peterson, G. W., Reardon, R. C., & Lenz, J. G. (2000). Using readiness assessment to improve career services: A cognitive information processing approach. *The Career Development Quarterly, 49,* 146-174.

Sampson, J. P., Jr., Reardon, R. C., Peterson, G. W., & Lenz, J. G. (2004). *Career counseling and services.* Belmont, CA: Thompson.

Sampson, J.P., Jr., Shy, J., & Cooley, J. (2007). *Client use of Internet websites as an information resource for problem solving.* Tallahassee, FL: Florida State University, Center for the Study of Technology in Counseling and Career Development.

Shahnasarian, M. (2005). *Decision time: A guide to career enhancement* (3rd ed.). Broken Arrow, OK: National Career Development Association.

Super, D. E. (1980). A life-span, life-space approach to career development. *Journal of Vocational Behavior, 16,* 282–298.

U. S. Department of Labor, Bureau of Labor Statistics. (2010–2011). *Occupational outlook handbook.* Retrieved from http://www.bls.gov/oco/

Chapter 2
USE OF THE INTERNET IN FACE-TO-FACE AND DISTANCE COUNSELING

Online resources can be used in a variety of ways to support career development. Career practitioners in traditionally face-to-face settings or who deliver services completely online may use resources on the Internet during the session or for outside session work. In this chapter, we will review potential ways for using the Internet in the career planning process and describe a model for integrating Internet use with career counseling.

Options for Using the Internet to Support Career Planning

The Internet provides relatively easy access to a wide diversity of career planning resources and services, both in a practitioner supported and self-help modes. Table 2.1 shows how websites and interactions among practitioners and clients can be related.

Websites provide opportunities to promote learning through the use of specific career-assessment and information websites assigned as homework between face-to-face or distance

Table 2.1 Options for Using Websites and Interactions Among Individuals

> **Using the Internet to Access Career Planning Resources**
> - Internet websites used by clients as homework in face-to-face career counseling
> - Internet websites used by clients as homework in distance career counseling
> - Internet websites used collaboratively by clients and practitioners during a face-to-face career counseling session
> - Internet websites used collaboratively by clients and practitioners during a distance career counseling session
> - Internet websites used by individuals to access self-help career assessment and information resources
> - E-portfolios in which students house evidence of their skills, experiences, resume and even video clips of an interview which can then be accessed by a career practitioner and/or employer (Garis & Dalton, 2007)
> - Distance career counseling using the Internet to allow communication among practitioners and clients
> - Social networking among individuals making career choices with or without assistance from a career practitioner
> - Distance and face-to-face career courses using the Internet to allow communication among instructors and students

counseling sessions. A career practitioner or career center may create an online repository that organizes information and resources for client use in career problem solving (Epstein & Lenz, 2008). The selection of specific websites depends on the characteristics and needs of the client. Chapter 6 describes assessment and information websites that can be assigned as homework. If a series of websites are used, an individual learning plan can help clients sequence. The learning plan can evolve as the client's needs change (Sampson, 2008).

Using websites during counseling (either face-to-face or at a distance) has the potential to make important contributions to individuals' career planning. During a counseling session, the practitioner can locate specific content on a website that relates to the client's needs. This type of immediate access to information allows for a "teachable moment" which may increase the effectiveness of using career assessments and information and model how to locate and evaluate career information. Having such a "teachable moment" provides practitioners and clients with the opportunity to immediately process and apply what they are learning. A practitioner could then send the link or information electronically to the client. This may be very useful, as it is sometimes difficult for individuals to later reconstruct with a practitioner what they learned several days earlier (Sampson & Bloom, 2001).

Individuals' use of web-based career assessments and information can prompt face-to-face or distance career counseling. Another option for providing counseling is to have a help button on a website that allows individuals to gain access to a practitioner immediately via the telephone or the Internet for a brief advising interaction while the person is using a career resource (synchronous communication). Another option would be to send a question to a career practitioner using a generic web-based email application (asynchronous communication). Here again, the immediacy of the interaction between the practitioner and the individual using the website provides a potentially powerful "teachable moment."

Websites delivering career assessment and information resources have a long history of being used on a self-help basis. As stated in Chapter 5 on ethical issues, successful use of a website is dependent on individuals having sufficient readiness for career planning to make effective use of the sites. (See http://www.career.fsu.edu/techcenter/designing_career_services/basic_concepts/index.html for additional details). The ability of individuals to get relatively immediate help from a practitioner when needed makes readiness problems and website use less problematic.

Distance career counseling uses technology to provide brief or longer-term counseling when the practitioner and one or more clients are in different locations. Recent advances in technology have shown an explosion in the area of social networking sites. Some sites (such as LinkedIn) have job-related networking and career information as their main purpose, but other strictly social sites are also being used for similar purposes. Chapter 5 describes the use of social networking sites in career services.

Career development facilitator training and undergraduate and graduate courses most always include the review of career-related websites as a portion of the training. Participants in these courses are often asked to use websites to write about a specific occupation or to complete online career assessments. Other activities might include evaluating career-related websites (Zalaquett & Osborn, 2007) or a career information safari in which students are asked to locate different sources of career information such as a sample advertisement, blog, wiki entry, or video along with traditional sources of career information (http://www.debosborn.com/teaching_examples/information_assignment.doc). As a follow-up discussion, the instructor could ask students to evaluate the information on quality, validity, and so forth. Additional information on distance career counseling is provided in the following section.

Distance Career Counseling

Distance career counseling "involves the provision of brief or longer-term individual counseling to clients via the telephone or the Web that is often augmented by the use of career assessments and information available on the Internet" (Sampson, 2008, p. 15). An example of an established career counseling business that is offered via distance is Readyminds (http://www.readyminds.com). Potential clients are offered a menu of service options and paired with a trained career counselor who works with them using online assessments, email, a drop box, and telephone.

Communication in distance career counseling can be asynchronous or synchronous. Asynchronous communication occurs sequentially with a time delay between interactions. Emailing, tweeting, blogging, and texting are examples of asynchronous communication. Synchronous communication provides interaction between two people without delay. Text chatting, talking (with or without a visual image), and communicating with sign language are examples of synchronous communication. Interaction in a virtual world using avatars is also a type of synchronous communication. However, this type of interaction in counseling is not common at present. While synchronous communication is faster, thus allowing more interaction in a given period of time, the time delays in asynchronous communication allow a period of reflection before responding.

Distance counseling has the potential to assist individuals who may be underserved with face-to-face services or who may prefer remote assistance. For some persons, receiving counseling at a distance is *necessity;* for other individuals, it is used for the sake of *convenience.* Distance counseling is a necessity for (a) persons with disabilities who have substantial mobility problems that make it difficult to travel, (b) individuals who live in remote geographic areas who do not have reasonable access to career resources and services, (c) individuals who seek access to practitioners in other geographic areas who have the specialized expertise they need, and (d) individuals who have been reluctant to seek counseling and find the relative anonymity of the Internet to be a safe place to start receiving help. Distance counseling is a convenience for individuals who want to access counseling outside of normal business hours or who want to receive assistance at their place of residence or work (Sampson & Bloom, 2001).

The skills required of the practitioner, the importance of the counseling relationship, and the basic nature of the counseling process are similar for technology-assisted distance counseling and for face-to-face counseling. However, some differences do exist. For example, practitioners and clients working at a distance need to develop additional skills in identifying emotions when visual data from the client and the practitioner are unavailable. Saunders (2007) gave several recommendations for the practitioner to consider when determining whether to provide distance counseling. Some of these include:

- developing a comprehensive business plan that describes what adaptations to the existing private practice will be necessary for distance counseling to be successful;
- determining how screening of potential clients will occur, and the criteria to be used for determining of readiness and appropriateness for engaging in distance counseling;
- identifying which distance counseling tools will be used;
- creating an explanation of distance counseling services for clients, including security, confidentiality, and other legal/ethical information;
- seeking regular supervision and evaluation of services; and
- pilot-testing the distance counseling service before publicly offering services, to build skills and work through technological issues.

17

The practitioner may perceive that the client is not benefiting from distance career counseling as a result of the client not following through with homework assignments, not showing any progress in career planning, and/or expressing reservations about interacting with the practitioner at a distance. If this is the case, it is imperative that the practitioner make an appropriate referral to a qualified practitioner in the client's geographic area.

Categorizing distance counseling as telephone-based or Internet-based is becoming less relevant due to the increasing integration of the telephone and the Internet. Examples of this integration include the capability to talk with and view another person while exchanging files and website links using smart phones and web-based videoconferencing sites (such as Skype). The transmission of digital data provides the basis for both the telephone and the Internet. For additional information on distance counseling, see http://www.career.fsu.edu/techcenter/computer_applications/bibliographies/index.html or refer to Malone, Miller, and Walz (2007).

A Model for Integrating Counseling and Website Use

Chapter 1 examined how assessment and information contributes to career decision making. Clients often use assessment and information resources as homework in counseling. Completing homework between counseling sessions can help clients gain or clarify knowledge about themselves and their potential options that can then be used in problem solving.

The websites described in Chapter 5 can be used by clients as a resource for counseling homework. While most individuals use the Internet on a self-help basis, others have lower readiness for career planning and need to use the Internet within the context of a counseling relationship in order to make effective use of the overwhelming number of resources that are available. In order to help clients obtain maximum benefits from using the Internet as a homework resource, parsimonious models are needed that integrate this technology with counseling.

A four-step counseling process can be used to promote effective client use of a website (Sampson, Shy, & Cooley, 2008). This model is relevant for both face-to-face and distance counseling. The four steps are (a) screening, (b) recommending, (c) orienting, and (d) follow-up. The counseling relationship begins with the screening process and is maintained through the subsequent steps.

Purpose of Each Step

Each of the steps have a purpose, including:

1. **Screening:** to determine the likelihood that using online assessments, information resources, and opportunities for interaction with others will help the client in career problem solving.

2. **Recommending:** to suggest Web-based assessments, information resources, and opportunities to communicate with others that are appropriate for the client's needs.

3. **Orienting:** to help ensure that clients make effective use of a website by promoting a realistic understanding of the potential benefits, limitations, and functioning of the site in relation to their needs.

3. **Follow-up:** to help ensure that clients have appropriately used website assessments, information sources, and opportunities for interacting with others to meet previously identified needs.

Counseling interventions and potential outcomes for each of the four steps in the model are presented in Table 2.2. The strategies described in this paper can also be applied to instruction where teachers in career courses have the opportunity to interact with their students on an individual basis.

Table 2.2 Counselor Interventions and Potential Client Outcomes

	1. Screening	2. Recommending	3. Orienting	4. Follow-Up
Counselor Interventions	• Clarify the career counseling concern. • Collaborate on counseling goals and need for assessment, information or interacting with others. • Is homework appropriate? • Determine client readiness for problem solving (see Chapter 1). • Collaboratively determine amount of practitioner support needed. • Decide on the appropriateness of using the Internet as a resource.	• Determine website that meets client needs. • Select appropriate website components, sequence activities, and monitor client pacing. • Collaboratively develop a written plan for using online resources. • Identify which needs might be best met by other information sources.	• Review written plan. • Review website elements (site navigation, help keys, privacy limits, supplemental information, estimated time required). • Consider client readiness to effectively use website. • Provide orientation information in print format for easy reference. • Encourage time for reflection over website interaction and results. • Help client learn to differentiate between high and low quality sites by pointing out indicators that the site is providing valid information and resources.	• Ask client to describe the experience and note any problems that need resolving. • As appropriate, reinforce client's information seeking behavior. • Help clients review progress towards meeting career needs. • Address any inappropriate use of the website or negative thinking about learning. • Recommend appropriate further resources and services as needed. • Discuss how learning resulted from website use can be applied to future problem solving. • Focus on balancing the conversation. Especially when interpreting assessment results, it can be very easy for the practitioner to dominate the conversation (Osborn & Zunker, 2006).
Potential Client Outcomes	• Established a good relationship with the practitioner. • Concluded that the practitioner understands the situation and is capable of helping. • Clarified his or her problems and counseling goals. • Concluded that the practitioner will be available to provide the type and amount of support that he or she needs. • Achieved a general understanding of how assessments, information, and interacting with others via the Internet may help with problem solving. • Decided that the Internet provides an appropriate source of assessments, information, or interaction with others.	• Achieved an understanding of how his or her needs can be potentially met by website use. • Formulated an initial plan for using the website, as well as any other appropriate resources. • Concluded that the practitioner is competent and available to help him or her make effective use of the website.	• Achieved a greater understanding of how specific portions of the website might be used to meet his or her needs. • Perceived him or herself as capable of successfully using the portions of the website that the practitioner has recommended. • Continued to conclude that the practitioner is competent and available to help him or her make effective use of the website.	• Fully used the web-based assessments, information sources, or opportunity to interact with others to meet his or her needs. • Evaluated the amount of progress that has been attained in meeting his or her needs, as well as identifying other resources and services that may meet his or her current needs. • Understood content and navigation of the website well enough to be better prepared to use portions of another website to meet similar needs. • Continued to conclude that the practitioner is competent and available to help him or her make current or future use of the website.

The interventions in Table 2.2 are meant to be guidelines for what the counselor should address at that step of the model. The outcomes listed are what a client may potentially experience as a result of achieving a specific step. While we believe that each of the guidelines listed in the counselor intervention section of the table should be addressed, the outcomes will be unique to each client.

Client Readiness

In Chapter 1, we discussed the impact of client readiness on the outcome of any intervention. Client readiness is a key component to be considered at each stage of this model as well. At the selection step, the career practitioner should work with the client to choose the most appropriate tool to meet the need. For example, a supercomputer could be used to determine the sum of 2 + 2, however, a simpler tool of one's fingers would likely prove less frustrating, less scary, and take less time. Similarly, while a comprehensive career website might allow the client to complete multiple inventories and cross-reference the results with several directories, this could be overwhelming to a client who is at a lower level of readiness and who simply wants to see what career options are associated with a certain field of study. Our goal should be to use the right tool for the given need. Thus, as a practitioner is screening and recommending online resources, the client's readiness to use the tool should be at the forefront of the consideration.

Readiness should be revisited at the time the client is going to use the online resource. Clients with low readiness for problem solving will need more careful orientation to the website. More effective orientation for persons with low readiness may reduce the anxiety associated with using a website, leading to more complete and more effective use of a site. Also, clients with low readiness for problem solving may benefit from practitioner modeling of information-seeking behavior by briefly demonstrating a pathway for moving through the site to obtain an assessment, an information resource, or an opportunity for personal communication. It is important, however, to avoid overwhelming the client with more orientation information than the client can understand and use at one time. Clients with high readiness may need only minimal orientation to the website, in some cases relying principally on the orientation and help features included on the site.

Before discussing the results in the follow-up step, the career practitioner should once again revisit client readiness to process the experience. If a client has spent two hours on a website, it might be better to schedule another time for the processing of the information and the experience. When the follow-up session begins, the career practitioner should be aware of other internal and external cues about the client's readiness to discuss the results. A client who has received important news about a personal issue might want to first spend time discussing that topic instead of diving into the results of the online activity.

Selecting, Sequencing, and Pacing Interventions

Once a client has been screened (step 1) and it has been determined that an online intervention may be beneficial, the next step (step 2) involves selecting and sequencing website content and features that meet client needs, while pacing client use of the site at a rate that is congruent with the client's readiness for career problem solving.

- *Selecting* includes identifying specific web-based assessments, information content, and opportunities to communicate with others that are likely to meet a client's needs. Some client needs will be addressed with one portion of a website, whereas other needs will be addressed by having the client use two or more portions of a website.

- *Sequencing* addresses the order that clients use website content and features. For example, before learning about strategies for changing behavior, clients may benefit from understanding the factors that contribute to the problem.

- *Pacing* identifies how fast clients use website resources and how many resources clients effectively use at any one time. Pacing can vary depending on client readiness, evolving slowly for clients with low readiness, where resources are presented in small achievable units. Clients with a high level of readiness for problem solving can use several resources relatively quickly. Structuring the initial and subsequent use of a website is especially important for clients with low readiness for career problem solving.

One way to help the client manage the information of which online tool is being used for what purpose and at what time, is to develop a written plan, which can be as simple as a sequential list of assessments, information sources, and opportunities for interaction on a website, or as complete as an individual learning plan (Sampson, Reardon, Peterson, & Lenz, 2004). An example of a completed Individual Learning Plan is shown in Figure 2.1.

Figure 2.1 Example of a Completed Individual Learning Plan

Goal(s): #1 – To find occupations that match my interests
#2 – To learn about different occupations
#3 – To make a career decision

Activity	Purpose / Outcome	Estimated Time Commitment	Goal #	Priority
Take an online career assessment	To see which occupations match interests	1-2 hours	#1	1
Use O*NET and online Occupational Outlook Handbook	To learn about occupations	1-2 hours	#2	2
Compile information into a comparison table	To begin to narrow down options	1-2 hours	#3	3

Imagine that a person has several career needs. Perhaps in addition to the needs listed in the sample learning plan, the person also wants to work on a resume and find an international internship opportunity. Without having some type of written plan, it is possible that one or more of the client's goals could be lost in the process, or that the client could become overwhelmed with the number of resources and activities available to meet each need. The sample learning plan in Figure 2.1 applies structure to what can feel like a very chaotic process. The plan can vary depending on client readiness, evolving slowly for clients with low readiness, presenting learning resources in small achievable units.

Summary

This chapter began with a description of how websites can be used in the delivery of online and face-to-face career services. Distance career counseling is then described as an approach to extending the availability of counseling services to individuals in almost any location. The chapter ends with a four-step model for integrating Internet websites in face-to-face and distance counseling. Emphasis is given to client readiness and how a practitioner might select, sequence and pace the use of online interventions.

References

Epstein, S. A., & Lenz, J. G. (2008). *Developing and managing career resources.* Broken Arrow, OK: National Career Development Association.

Garis, J. W., & Dalton, J. C. (Eds.). (2007). *E-Portfolios: Emerging opportunities for student affairs.* New Directions in Student Services, No. 119. San Francisco: Jossey-Bass.

Malone, J. E., Miller, R. M., & Walz, G. R. (Eds.) (2007). *Distance counseling: Expanding the counselor's reach.* Ann Arbor, MI: Counseling Outfitters, LLC.

Osborn, D. S., & Zunker, V. G. (2006). *Using assessment results for career development* (7th ed.). Pacific Grove, CA: Brooks/Cole Publishing Company.

Sampson, J. P., Jr. (2004, June). Readiness for effective use of computer-assisted career guidance systems: A preliminary multidimensional model. In J. Harris-Bowlsbey (Chair). *"International Perspectives on Career Development."* Paper presented at an International Symposium of the International Association for Educational and Vocational Guidance and the National Career Development Association, San Francisco, CA.

Sampson, J. P., Jr. (2008). *Designing and implementing career programs: A handbook for effective practice.* Broken Arrow, OK: National Career Development Association.

Sampson, J. P., Jr., & Bloom, J. W. (2001). The potential for success and failure of computer applications in counseling and guidance. In D. C. Locke, J. Myers, & E. L. Herr (Eds.), *The handbook of counseling* (pp. 613–627). Thousand Oaks, CA: Sage Publications.

Sampson, J. P., Jr., Peterson, G. W., Reardon, R. C., & Lenz, J. G. (2000). Using readiness assessment to improve career services: A cognitive information processing approach. *The Career Development Quarterly,* 49, 146–174.

Sampson, J. P., Jr., Reardon, R. C., Peterson, G. W., & Lenz, J. G. (2004). *Career counseling and services: A cognitive information processing approach.* Pacific Grove, CA Brooks/Cole.

Sampson, J.P., Jr., Shy, J., & Cooley, J. (2008). *A four-step model for integrating counseling and web site use.* Tallahassee, FL: Florida State University, Center for the Study of Technology in Counseling and Career Development.

Saunders, D. E. (2007). A step-by-step approach for adopting and using distance counseling as a private practitioner. In J. F. Malone, R. M. Miller, & G. R. Walz (Eds.), *Distance counseling: Expanding the counselor's reach and impact,* 75-89. Ann Arbor, MI: Counseling Outfitters, LLC.

Zalaquett, C., & Osborn, D. S. (2007). Fostering counseling students' career information literacy through a comprehensive career web site. *Counselor Education and Supervision,* 46, 162–171.

CHAPTER 3
DEVELOPING A COMPREHENSIVE VIRTUAL CAREER CENTER

This chapter is intended to help practitioners explore the possibilities of contributing to and using comprehensive virtual career centers. Practitioners who are technologically capable may design a virtual career center and also be responsible for uploading and managing site content. Practitioners who have technical support can contribute to the creation of virtual career centers by providing content and suggesting design features to technical staff members who create them. They can also use virtual career centers as a vehicle for delivering counseling interventions. This chapter describes the two basic components of a virtual career center, indicates how these may be used to assist students or clients, and cites their potential limitations.

Virtual career centers can be a necessity or a convenience in the delivery of career resources and services, as noted in standards developed by the National Board for Certified Counselors and the Center for Credentialing and Education (http://www.nbcc.org). A virtual career center can be a necessity when geographic distance or a disability limits access to other career resources and services. A virtual career center can provide convenience when distance counseling can be scheduled outside of traditional service delivery hours or delivered at a place of residence or employment.

The two main components of a virtual career center are (a) an organized website that provides linkages to career resources (such as the resources described in Chapter 5) and (b) distance counseling or synchronous career workshops (described previously in Chapter 2). A *website* is the total collection of resources maintained by an individual or an organization, including a home page, internal links to content pages, and external links to other related sites. A career service website can deliver assessments, information, and instructional resources in support of individuals and clients who are in the process of making career decisions.

Some basic components of all virtual career centers include:
- Career center/site name
- Mission statement/goals/objectives of the center
- Services provided (both online and face-to-face, if the center is also brick and mortar)
- Site map
- *About us* link that describes who is providing services and their qualifications
- Contact information
- Date the site was last updated

Some other optional components might include:
- Chat or email option
- Resource guides
- Links to other sites (and a description of how links are chosen/evaluated)
- Blog
- Events or calendar
- Search function
- Keyword index

- Job bank
- Links to social networking sites on which the center is located

- Pages and resources of interest to specific groups
- Publications and newsletters

A virtual career center may have many other components; these should be specific to the services the center offers and the clientele it serves.

Career Center Websites and the Career Planning Process

Career service websites can support numerous elements of the career planning process. Clients can confirm that they have a need to make a career decision by reviewing topics that stimulate their thinking about potential career problems. They can learn about and/or reevaluate self-information by completing online assessments. Many assessments also help users to generate occupational alternatives. Database searches allow the generation of occupational, educational, training, and employment alternatives by relating various personal characteristics and preferences to available career options. The site can provide access to information about identified alternatives by linking to internal and external sources of occupational, educational/training, and employment information. This information can be used to learn about and narrow the options being considered, leading ultimately to a career choice. A choice can then be implemented by accessing the many employment resources on the Internet to organize a job campaign, research employing organizations, create resumes and cover letters, and prepare for job interviews. (See http://www.rileyguide.com/ for additional details on job search strategies).

This process can overlay a generic decision-making cycle. For example, a person needing to make a career decision can use the CASVE decision-making cycle from cognitive information processing theory (Sampson, Reardon, Peterson, & Lenz, 2004). This person might use online resources to work through this decision as illustrated in the following model in Figure 3.1.

Figure 3.1 Applying the CASVE Cycle to Online Resource Use

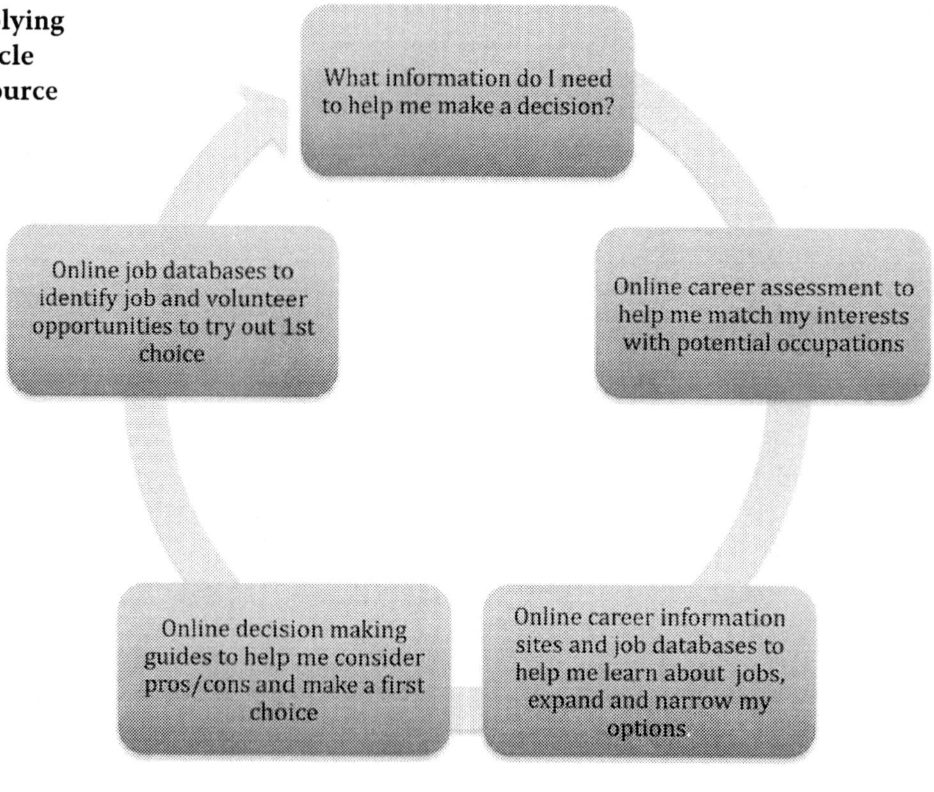

What information do I need to help me make a decision?

Online career assessment to help me match my interests with potential occupations

Online career information sites and job databases to help me learn about jobs, expand and narrow my options

Online decision making guides to help me consider pros/cons and make a first choice

Online job databases to identify job and volunteer opportunities to try out 1st choice

The Internet can also be used to communicate with prospective employers. Chapter 5 provides a comprehensive listing of sites that can be used to support the career planning process described above.

Career Websites for Self-Help or to Support Counseling

Individuals can use a career service website on a self-help basis or as one component of career counseling. For use as a self-help resource, the site must be designed so that the individual can understand (a) the potential usefulness of the site, including how elements of the site contribute to career planning, (b) how the site functions, (c) potential follow-up activities, and (d) the circumstances when practitioner assistance may be needed. The individual is responsible for deciding how much, and the way in which, the site will be used. The client or student is also responsible for deciding whether counseling is subsequently needed to make an appropriate career choice.

For use as a resource to support face-to-face and distance counseling, the site should be designed so that the client can understand how it functions. The practitioner is responsible for determining client readiness for use of site content, orienting the client to content that relates to specific needs, and following up with the client to determine if needs have been met. The same website resources used on a self-help basis can also be used as homework assignments in counseling. (See Chapters 1 and 2 for a more complete discussion of the use of sites as homework in counseling). Some clients use information more effectively by writing down and reflecting on what they are learning. For example, a client might be asked to research three occupations using an online career site such as O*NET or the online version of the *Occupational Outlook Handbook* (See Chapter 5). A practitioner could create a personalized table with a client during a session and then share the table electronically with the client. The client's homework would be to complete the table using assigned websites and bring it back or send it to the practitioner before the next session. A sample occupational table is provided below in Table 3.1.

Another example of an occupational comparison sheet can be found at https://sites.google.com/site/debbieosborn/teaching-tools.

Table 3.1 Sample Occupational Comparison Table

	Occupation 1	Occupation 2	Occupation 3
Does it involve working with people, things, data, or ideas?			
How much $ will I make on average?			
How much education will I need?			

In addition to serving individuals and clients at a distance, career center sites can also contribute to the traditional functions of a career center. They can be used to market center services to potential clients by making users more aware of how these services can meet specific career planning needs. For example, a user who is reviewing resources on resume writing can learn of career center workshops that are scheduled on this topic by reading information contained on an internal link. Through marketing, individuals using resources on a career center site can become clients seeking traditional career services. A second contribution of career center sites to the traditional functioning of a career center is to organize external websites in a career library. Rather than using search engines or bookmarks in a browser, a career center site can present preselected, high-quality links related to well-defined user needs. In this way, links to external websites are simply one more resource available in a career center library.

Use of a Career Center or School Website by Level of Service Delivery

All levels of service delivery can include the use of websites. The career center or school website should be available in the career resource room to facilitate individuals' access to appropriate resources for the populations being served. The website could be set as the home page, included on a list of favorites, or bookmarked. By having the website available on all computers in a career resource room, individuals can become familiar with the content and use of the site. When practitioners and other staff members model website use, individuals' information-seeking behaviors can be enhanced (Sampson, 2008).

It is essential that when individuals using the site on a self-help basis experience difficulty, the potential benefits of talking with a practitioner are clearly indicated (Offer, Sampson, & Watts, 2001). One example of a well organized online career center library with multiple career-related links can be seen at http://www.career.fsu.edu/library.

Alternative Models for Website Development

While all websites deliver information, resources, or services, sites vary in the extent to which a focus is placed on user needs. A continuum exists in designs from less to more need-based.

Resource-Based Sites

Resource-based sites are typically organized around the content delivered on the site. Lists of internal content links and external links are provided with or without accompanying descriptive statements. Users choose resources and services they perceive to meet their needs. Resource-based sites are most appropriate for experienced users (Sampson, Carr, Panke, Arkin, Minvielle, & Vernick, 2003).

Potential advantages of resource-based designs include the following: (a) users who are familiar with site content can quickly find appropriate resources and services, (b) development costs are lower because less staff effort and time are required to develop the site, and (c) adding new content is simpler because only titles, perhaps including short descriptions, of links are required. A potential disadvantage of a resource-based design is that it may be more difficult for users to select resources and services that meet their needs if a resource title and description do not provide enough information to help them match needs and resources. The process of matching user needs to resources often takes a skilled practitioner with substantial training and practice. Resource-based sites often require users to be able to employ this skill without assistance from a skilled practitioner. Resource-based sites are most appropriate for those who know exactly the name and type of resource they need to answer a specific question, or for return visitors to a website.

Need-Based Sites

Need-based sites are typically organized around audience members and their needs. A need-based design includes three separate levels. The first level is a list of potential audience members (such as students, parents, and employers). The second level includes descriptions of potential needs for specific audience members. The third level lists resources that potentially meet the needs of specific audience members. For each resource identified, a description is provided along with a statement of the potential outcomes that may result from using the resource. Need-based sites are most appropriate for novice users.

Potential advantages of need-based designs include the following: (a) users view only those resources that relate to their needs, creating a site that is easier to navigate; (b) users are less likely to become overwhelmed with information by providing them with access to a few well-supported, carefully selected, high-quality external links; (c) users are encouraged to seek help from a practitioner when suggestions for assistance are included; and (d) users may identify relevant needs that they were not aware of previously by reading need statements. The greater amount of development time needed to conceptualize related audiences, needs, and resources is a potential disadvantage of need-based designs. Another disadvantage is the difficulty of operationalizing the expert knowledge of practitioners. A third disadvantage may occur if there is no option for returning visitors to quickly find what they need. A needs-based design should consider return visitors and include a link for them so that they can navigate through the system quickly.

Creating content for a need-based site requires asking three key questions: (a) Who does (or should) the site serve? (b) What are the needs of these users? (c) What resources are available (or should be available) to meet user needs? Remembering past interactions with clients can help practitioners clarify user needs and subsequently connect users to appropriate resources and services. By incorporating the expertise of practitioners, the site can be an "intelligent" approach to delivering resources and services that are more likely to meet user needs.

It is also possible to combine the features of need-based and resource-based sites through the use of resource-based tools, such as a site map, site index, and a search mechanism. These features are especially useful for more advanced users. For additional information on need-based website designs, see http://www.career.fsu.edu/techcenter/computer_applications/need-based_web_sites.html. For an example of a career center website design that integrates need and resource-based designs, see http://www.career.fsu.edu. Guidelines for implementing websites are provided by Sampson, Carr, Panke, Arkin, Vernick, and Minvielle (2004).

Potential Benefits and Limitations of Career Center Websites

Possible Benefits

Career center websites offer many potential benefits. The first is convenience. Individuals do not have to leave their office or home to access career information and resources during regular business hours, but can access the site when they are ready. Vast amounts of information can be stored online, leading to less repetition by a career practitioner who can provide a face-to-face or online client with information. The career site can be used to enhance face-to-face or online career counseling by asking the client to utilize certain aspects of the site.

Potential Limitations

Career center websites, whether used at a distance or in a career center, are not without their limitations. They can be difficult to navigate, making it less likely that users can match resources and services to their needs. They can lack the content that users need to fully complete the career planning process. If users are unable to locate the resources and services they need, they may erroneously conclude that they are incapable of being helped or that a career service is not able to meet their needs. Some users might not be ready to successfully take a career assessment online and interpret it themselves, or to use career information in a meaningful way. Career center sites may also be associated with the problems and ethical issues discussed in Chapter 6. Not only do these problems and ethical issues potentially compromise the site's effectiveness, individuals and clients may be actually harmed as a result of using a career center site that is inappropriately designed and used.

Summary

In this chapter, we discussed the development of a comprehensive virtual career center. We explored how the virtual career center could be used as the main vehicle for providing career services or as a way to augment services provided by a brick and mortar career center. We discussed how a virtual career center with appropriate links might be used to help someone through the career decision-making process, and how the site can be used to enhance various levels of service delivery. Last, we discussed potential benefits and limitations of virtual career centers.

References

Offer, M., Sampson, J. P., Jr., & Watts, A. G. (2001). *Career services technology and the future.* Manchester, United Kingdom: Higher Education Careers Services Unit and the National Institute for Careers Education and Counselling.

Sampson, J. P., Jr. (2008). *Designing and implementing career programs: A handbook for effective practice.* Broken Arrow, OK: National Career Development Association.

Sampson, J. P., Jr., Carr, D. L., Panke, J., Arkin, S., Minvielle, M., & Vernick, S. H. (2003). *Design strategies for need-based Internet websites in counseling* (Technical Report No. 28). Tallahassee, FL: Florida State University, Center for the Study of Technology in Counseling and Career Development. Retrieved from http://www.career.fsu.edu/techcenter/computer_applications/need-based_web_sites.html

Sampson, J. P., Jr., Carr, D. L., Panke, J., Arkin, S., Vernick, S. H., & Minvielle, M. (2004). Implementing Internet websites in counseling services. In J. Bloom & G. Walz (Eds.), *Cybercounseling and cyberlearning: Strategies and resources for the millennium* (2nd ed., pp. 247–257). Greensboro, NC: American Counseling Association and ER Clearinghouse on Counseling and Student Services.

Sampson, J. P., Jr., Reardon, R. C., Peterson, G. W., & Lenz, J. G. (2004). *Career counseling and services: A cognitive information processing approach.* Pacific Grove, CA Brooks/Cole.

CHAPTER 4
USE OF SOCIAL NETWORKING SITES IN DELIVERING CAREER SERVICES

In the old days of job searching, "networking" was the way to find access to the hidden job market. Friends and acquaintances of one's family and friends became the path for finding a specific type of job in a specific company or geographical location. With the explosion of Web 2.0, online social networking possibilities have become far more extensive than traditional networking could ever have offered. With traditional networking, a person would be dependent upon which contacts the other person shared. With social networking websites, after setting up an online profile and inviting a handful of friends to join, one's network will likely experience exponential growth within a very short time.

Purpose of Online Social Networking

The purpose of social networking sites is to connect users. On these sites, users create a profile, and provide as much personal and professional information as they wish. They may also upload photos, videos, and links. Individuals can also easily create weblogs, also known as blogs, in which they can journal about their thoughts and reactions to events or nonevents in their lives. The purpose of Twitter (described in detail later) is to allow members to micro-blog (up to 140 characters) about their lives in what are called "tweets." In social networks, members invite individuals to join their network or to "friend" them. This process connects two individuals with the added benefit of allowing the newly linked members to see all the other "friends" in each other's network. While individuals can choose any name they would like for their profile, using one's real name is suggested so that employers and others searching for the individual can easily locate the person.

Research on Online Social Networking Sites

Many universities maintain a presence on social networking sites (SNSs). While research is still very sparse on the use of SNSs, what we do know confirms what the media and sites report—that millions of people, including students, are subscribed and regularly use these sites. The use of SNSs has also been related to college completion and social integration (Morris, Reese, Beck, & Mattis, 2010) and gains in social capital (Steinfield, Ellison, & Lampe, 2008).

Students may have different opinions than faculty and staff on the use of SNSs. In one study, researchers compared faculty and student usage of and attitudes towards SNSs and found that students were much more likely than faculty to use these sites and to be open about using these sites to support their classroom work (Roblyer, McDaniel, Webb, Herman, & Witty, 2010). Also, another study showed that while the majority of students had a "social networking presence" and were open to linking with the library through their SNSs, there was a large minority that responded negatively to that idea (Connell, 2009). The point for career practitioners to keep in mind is that there is a fine line between connecting and infringing.

Social or Professional Network?

One of the problems with these social networking sites is that a person might have "friends" who are friends and family, but also "friends" who are current coworkers or potential employers. The lines between personal and professional may quickly become blurred. Anecdotal evidence exists that it is becoming more common for employers to conduct online searches on applicants. Hiring decisions might be made prior to ever inviting an applicant for an interview based on information found posted about or by the individual. Two researchers (Kolek & Saunders, 2008) looked at Facebook profiles of students from a large public university and found that the majority of students had profiles, many containing large amounts of public information, including pictures of alcohol consumption. Clients should be aware that others may make assumptions about them based on information posted on SNSs. Kluemper and Rosen (2009) asked 378 judges to identify personality and other traits of six SNS profiles and found that the judges were able to accurately determine the "big-five" personality traits, intelligence, and performance based solely on information from the SNS profiles.

One potential answer to this dilemma is to have an account just for family and friends and another account for professional contacts. LinkedIn (described later) is an example of a professional social networking site. Connections can be made directly from one person to another, but the initiator has to have a common connection, such as work, school, or another person. An individual could also ask one of their contacts to foster an introduction. Another potential use of LinkedIn is to endorse someone, which is basically writing a brief letter of recommendation for that person that acts as a testimonial. In addition, a member can search companies and industries of interest, and find employees (current or former) who are connected to the member. The benefit is that the contact can pass the member's resume on to the right person in the company. Once again, the power is not in the resume itself but in the connection (or networking relationship) of the person who passes the resume along.

Social Networking Basics for Job Searching

Several key elements are required for using SNSs for job searching. These include creating a powerful profile, developing an online social network, and using status updates strategically.

Creating a Powerful Profile

In order to begin networking on an online social network, an individual has to develop a profile. A profile can best be described as an introduction page, where a person gives a brief synopsis of who they are and what they have accomplished. Many online sources indicate that a large number of employers are either directly or through sourcing firms always scanning for passive candidates, i.e., those who already have a position but who may be willing to leave if presented with an attractive opportunity. This is the first page a potential employer sees, and thus what is included on this page and how it is presented is of great importance. While profile pages differ in what they allow, the following are general suggestions for creating a profile or landing page:

- Research companies of interest to identify keywords to use on the profile page.
- Take advantage of completing a professional summary to demonstrate your skills and work experience.

- Take advantage of a headline or branding statement, making it interesting and specific while not limiting too much. For example, instead of "counselor," say "career development practitioner and coach."

- Use multiple keywords that are likely to draw interest.

- If possible, select a main industry, as that may be a way some employers explore for potential candidates.

- Include all employers (past and present), as well as educational and training sites, and professional associations. If currently unemployed, consider using "open to opportunities" for current status, or "currently seeking ...".

- Include certifications, being as specific as possible, such as "Distance Career Counselor," or "MBA."

- Regularly update status, even if it is just a link to an updated blog. Don't post it and forget about it.

- As with any representation of oneself, make sure to proofread and spell check thoroughly.

- Consider adding a photo, but make sure it is professional and "reads" well. Seek honest feedback about reactions to the photo before settling on it. Recognize that just as with resumes, some may use a photograph to discriminate. The positive of using a photograph is that it "feels" more personal than text.

- Seek endorsements or recommendations from colleagues or previous employers and others. If an employer sees that a candidate is endorsed by a trusted "friend," this will likely impact the employer's thoughts about the candidate in a positive way.

- A profile should be made public (but keep private information private) so that employers or recruiters can easily find it. In addition, where possible, the URL should be customized to be the applicant's name. This extra step will ensure that the link will be listed when someone does a Google search of the candidate's name.

- Finally, create a signature that can then be automatically included in outgoing emails.

Like a person's name on their resume, a profile or landing page is the most important item on a social networking site. People make initial judgments on what is or is not present on that first page. Once an individual begins developing her or his social network, these contacts will begin looking at the individual's page. They may not return there for several weeks or months, so that first impression is critical.

Developing an Online Social Network

Once the profile is completed, the goal becomes developing one's social network. The first step is to determine the type of network that is desired. The purpose of sites such as LinkedIn have already been outlined by the developers. LinkedIn is a professional network. However, MySpace and Facebook are social networking sites that are increasingly being used for professional as well as social purposes. A potential problem occurs when an individual has high school friends, sorority/fraternity sisters and brothers, family members, coworkers, clients, and fellow professionals in the same network. How might a coworker or potential employer interpret the following?

- Pictures posted by a college roommate that show (or tag) the candidate using questionable judgment

- Friends' comments or pictures that are posted on the candidate's wall that indicate political party affiliation, and include curse words, discriminating attitudes, or comments about the candidate

- Groups the candidate or people the individual "follows" that might be offensive (such as prolife or prochoice, Democratic or Republican Party, and so forth)

Some sites allow the individual to limit what individual "friends" see and others do not. The decision on how authentic a person decides to be with posting information about his or her social and personal life is a personal preference. However, if individuals find that they are not getting the results desired, the career practitioner might encourage them to rethink their strategy on what to share publicly.

Joining groups is a great way to increase one's network. Some useful groups might include alumni associations and past or present employers. On some SNSs, one can become a "fan" of an employer or celebrity, social interest groups, groups focusing on hobbies, or supporters of different causes. The candidate should carefully evaluate the potential positives and negatives of joining each group. People make initial judgments on what is shown, and these judgments are not always correct. While the candidate who tries to avoid posting anything controversial may be seen as bland, the candidate who goes overboard with these types of posts, is likely to be seen as a driver of a car that is covered with bumper stickers, insensitive and feeling the need to broadcast his or her opinions, whether wanted or not, to the world.

It is possible to quickly increase one's network through these sites. Each friend that is added has his or her own network of friends who are now available to the individual. In looking at friends' contacts, some have 500 or more "friends." Is this even possible? Is it possible to have too many friends? Perhaps so, if one is referring to the true meaning of the word "friend." It would be near impossible to read 500, 300, or even 100 postings by individual friends and to make regular contributions to their pages. However, the job searcher should consider all of their SNSs as a potential job-search network. A person with a network of 10 friends will probably have fewer opportunities through networking than a person who has 50 friends, although quality may trump quantity. Still, a job searcher might post a question on her or his profile such as, "I would really love to work as a _____(job title)_____ in company _____(company name)_____ . Would you mind asking your friends if they know of how to break into that industry, or if they know of someone I could talk with in that company?" Who is more likely to find a positive response to this question the fastest, the person with ten contacts or the person with fifty?

Using Status Updates Strategically

Most social networking sites allow for members to post brief updates, blurbs, or tweets. This can be taken to the extreme, with people posting when they are going out to get the mail, going to bed, eating supper, and so forth. This same tool, however, can be a useful one for the job search. Members can use this tool to share that they are job searching and for what type of job, industry, or location. One could pose a question, such as

"Does anyone know ...

- about a company that might be hiring managers?,
- someone in graphic design in the Tampa area?, or
- somebody who is working in Company C?"

Most "friends" are willing to help if they possibly can. Other posts might be an update on interviews or when a change is made to a personal blog or website, including the link in the post. Some sites will allow for "tagging" friends. This can also be a useful strategy if not overused. By tagging a friend, the friend is alerted to that specific post and may be more likely to respond.

The Role of the Career Practitioner

Many of today's students are likely to know more about social networking sites than the average career practitioner or coach, but they may be less likely to know about general rules of networking or how SNSs might be used successfully for a job search. Older clients may be unfamiliar with social networking sites and may be limiting their job search by not including these sites as part of their job search strategy. The topic of SNSs should be presented as one of many strategies that should be utilized by today's job searcher. To rely or ignore SNSs completely in the job search would be closing oneself off to many potential employers.

Career practitioners can provide the following:

- Information on how to incorporate SNSs into one's job search plan
- Basic information on the key SNSs and job search strategies specific to each
- Suggestions on identifying, joining, and making the most of groups or becoming a "fan"
- Research strategies to learn about an industry, job positions, and employers (as well as a specific employer's competitors), utilizing traditional information as well as information that can only be found on SNSs
- Cautionary statements on what information, photos, videos, widgets, and so forth to post in a profile or bio, and information about using privacy settings
- Tips on how to create a personal website or blog, and information on what to include (and not include) on these, and whether or not to link to these
- Referring clients to their college or employer alumni association, as these may also have networking resources available
- Identifying how to increase one's online presence, to make one easy to be found by potential employers
- Information on how employers use different SNSs to locate potential candidates
- Managing an overall job search strategy, and knowing on which sites information is posted (so that it can be regularly updated)
- Advice on choosing "friends," as employers may be able to access their profiles and posts, and draw conclusions about the individual based on his or her associations
- Ideas on how to perform backwards company searches to identify employees who worked at the company at the same time the individual did. Specifically, the person doing the research would search for the employer and the names of people who have listed that employer as a place of employment at some time in their work history
- Suggestions for learning about interviewers through searching SNSs
- Applying general networking strategies to SNSs, such as:
  - setting networking goals
  - asking existing contacts to introduce to a desired contact
  - researching friends' and followers' backgrounds and biographies thoroughly to identify possible common interests or potential leads
  - focusing on relationship building with contacts
  - keeping good records of networking contacts
  - maintaining professional communications with all contacts
  - focusing on a balance of give and take in the relationship, not solely seeing or using the contact for what they can offer

A discussion about privacy issues, including who owns personal information, or the use of private information in advertising.

The key to remember is that the career practitioner does not need to be an expert in all the nuances of all the different types of technology currently available. There is a great degree of overlap among the tools, and many offer similar tools or widgets or applications, just calling them by a different name. The career practitioner should be aware of these general tools so as to be knowledgeable when speaking with the client and should seek to stay current on readings about developments in technology. The career practitioner is still likely to be the expert on traditional job-search and networking strategies, and many of these apply in the online social networking venue as well.

Facilitating Social Networking Between Career Practitioners and Clients

In addition, career practitioners can use SNSs to provide services and to connect with clients. Depending on the site, career practitioners can invite clients to become fans, friends, or followers. Real time and virtual events such as career fairs, workshops, videos about services or introducing staff, and links to webinars can be posted. Job listings can be listed, and discussions on job searching, choosing a major, or negotiating job interviews can be created. These sites offer the instant notification of the events, which is a benefit beyond a static website.

Career practitioners can also create group pages for members, such as a job search group, or an alumni group, or a career choice group. Group pages differ from group counseling in that the main function of these group pages is to provide information in an asynchronous manner, such as through posting on the main page or in a discussion board. Synchronous activities such as chatting is already possible through technologies such as Elluminate, GoTo Meeting, or similar programs that use Voice over Internet Protocol (VoIP), an online tool that allows for verbal chatting with multiple users over the computer instead of through the telephone or conference call. For today's client, being able to integrate technology into their counseling experience presents a tremendous opportunity, but raises equally important ethical questions.

Unique Ethical Issues and SNSs

The main issues regarding the use of social networking sites are confidentiality and privacy. The issues are similar to using any technology online, such as email. An individual must recognize that once a comment, picture, or video is posted, there is nothing to stop anybody from copying and pasting or publishing that information to the world. The candidate should take this fact into consideration before posting anything online. Many employers search out potential candidates online before making a decision about them. From the career practitioner's perspective, the question of ethics on the part of the employer is moot. This searching by employers is underway now, so the career practitioner's role is to alert students and clients to be aware that it is happening and to pay close attention to what they post online.

The issue of confidentiality is more critical when a career practitioner is providing counseling services online, and using these social networking sites to do it. If a practitioner hosts a group on a social site, how is confidentiality maintained? As a beginning step, the practitioner would need to coach individuals on how to keep their information private from others. Most of these sites do not allow verbal chatting, although Second Life does. Second Life uses avatars and does not allow "real names" to be chosen for the avatar, thus providing some degree of anonymity. However, there is nothing preventing members from sharing real names when chatting. It would be the practitioner's responsibility to make sure that protective measures are in place to provide privacy and to prevent "griefers" (i.e., individuals whose motivation is to aggravate and harass others in a virtual game or world) from listening into a counseling session. The same is true for online chats such as Elluminate and ILinc. The best ways to stay informed are (a) to ask the questions about security before using or purchasing the software, and (b) to spend time (or appoint someone else to spend time) regularly subscribing to and scanning technology blogs, podcasts, and websites. Venders of such sites often exhibit at professional conferences. In addition, talking with other practitioners or administrators who use these sites can also provide valuable insight. For additional information on ethical issues, see Chapter 6.

Sample Social Networking Sites

In looking at the most popular social networking sites, each has some type of career development or job searching group to join or follow, but this does not appear to be the best way to approach job searching. Many of the topics or posts seem to be on the "get rich quick" schemes or the "too good to be true" (so they're likely untrue) opportunities. The better approach is for individuals to use their primary and extended networks on these sites to connect to employers.

Facebook (www.facebook.com)

Used for both social and professional networking, Facebook is the most frequently used social networking site. According to the site, there are currently more than 500 million active users, spending over 700 billion minutes per month on Facebook, each user with an average of 130 friends. Fifty percent of the 500 million use Facebook daily. "Friendships" are initiated and either confirmed or ignored. Individuals provide information on a profile page and can upload links, photos, videos, or notes. Brief status updates are used to inform contacts of a person's activities for the moment or day. Notes can be sent and friends "tagged," both of which show up on their "wall" and in their email. Individuals can join groups and become fans of employers, organizations, movie stars, hobby sites, social causes, and the like. Instant chatting is also available, and privacy settings can be set to allow only certain information to be shared. Facebook offers several job-search applications or apps, including LinkUp (companies can post job openings on Fan Pages), virtual business cards, Inside Job, My LinkedIn Profile (connecting with a LinkedIn account), and Work With Us (by Jobvite). A client should be aware that personal information may be shared or sold with/to employers.

LinkedIn (www.linkedin.com)

LinkedIn is a professional social networking site boasting over 90 million users, with executives from all Fortune 500 companies, 170 industries, and a million companies represented. They provide a "gated access" to members, where contacts must know each other or be introduced to each other from a common contact. LinkedIn provides groups. In addition, members can write "endorsements" of other contacts which serve as brief letters of recommendation and can be seen by employers. Members can use an advanced search function to find contacts for a specific company, or browse through company profiles that also include current and previous employees who are contacts, using their Company Search tool. LinkedIn also allows companies to post jobs and individuals to link their blogs to their profile. If a person adds to his or her blog, it will be updated in the person's LinkedIn profile. Twitter Link also allows a person to import conversations from Twitter, which allows those not on Twitter to see that individual's tweets.

MySpace (www.myspace.com)

The focus of MySpace leans more towards the "social" side of SNSs, although it can be used as one aspect of a professional job search. Some of the features include bulletins (allowing for a post to all of one's "friends"), groups (providing a common page and a message board), instant messaging, forums, and classified ads.

Twitter (www.twitter.com)

In addition to following individual or organizational tweets, guests and members can also search for tweets about career, job, and interviewing. NCDA has a Twitter account at http://twitter.com/NCDA. Twellow is a Twitter tool that searches bios and URLs based on a variety of factors. One can search by company or industry, and the software provides a list of those people who are on Twitter. Other job search aids in Twitter include www.Twitterjobsearch.com (a job search engine that provides listings that match keywords), JobShouts (employers freely post job openings that are then tweeted to members), and JobAngels (also available on Facebook and LinkedIn, designed to motivate people to help just one other person find a job). Members should know that Twitter does sell information to third parties.

Blogger (www.blogger.com)

Blogger is a free weblog (blog) publishing system. Users can have their blog hosted free of charge on blogspot.com. An individual can use a blog to highlight skills, experiences, accomplishments, and reflections. Photos and videos can be uploaded, and individuals can choose to follow a person's blog. The blog can be linked to an individual's social networking site(s).

Omegle (http://omegle.com/)

Omegle is a site that allows for instant chatting with strangers from all over the world. A person can quit the conversation as quickly as they begin, and can share as much personal information as they wish. This may open opportunities for work internationally, but clients should be cautioned about divulging too much personal information without adequate proof of who the person is.

Second Life (www.secondlife.com)

Second Life (SL) is a virtual world in which members choose avatars to represent themselves and interact with other avatars from around the world. Many members are paid for services provided "in world" such as through designing "skins" or "builds" or even for providing counseling services. Corporations, universities, and professional organizations are represented in SL. Because the avatars represent real people, SL provides a unique opportunity to expand a social network.

Zimbio (http://www.zimbio.com/)

Zimbio is an online megamagazine made up of "wikizines" in which members can add or edit material on a specific topic. Ranked by alexa.com as one of the ten most popular magazines online, with more than 18 million readers each month, members can increase their visibility to potential employers and clients, as well as increase their expertise, by submitting articles, blog entries, or photographs or videos to a subject-specific wikizine.

Monster (www.monster.com)

Monster.com is one of the best known employment websites, where participants can search for jobs, post resumes, research occupations, and read advice columns focused on career planning. Readers can also join communities, such as the group for career women called "Excelle," and the "Govcentral" community, which is a very well-developed community with career guides, job opportunities, federal job fairs, and forums.

CareerBuilder (www.careerbuilder.com)

Known as the largest online job search website in the United States, CareerBuilder allows individuals to search for jobs, post resumes, have a resume critique, receive job recommendations from the site based on profile, and receive career advice. In addition, CareerBuilder has a professional community called BrightFuse, which is aimed at those in early career who are in the process of developing a professional network.

ZoomInfo (www.zoominfo.com)

ZoomInfo is a source boasting 50 million summaries of business professionals and 5 million company profiles that allows employers to locate "passive" job candidates, i.e., individuals who are currently employed and not looking for a job, but might be open to a new opportunity. ZoomInfo pulls public information on specific employees from various web sources, and also allows individuals to build a profile or add to its summaries. Ziggs and Notchup are similar sites.

Jobster (www.jobster.com)

Jobster is a comprehensive job search site that allows users to search job postings on their site as well as other job boards. Individuals create professional profiles, superstar tags (to highlight one's skills or experience), video profiles or resumes, and use social networking to increase their hiring potential.

Summary

To provide useful guidance on using SNSs in the job search or for career development, career practitioners and coaches must continually update their knowledge about how SNSs are being used by employers and candidates. This axiom translates into the need to regularly read information on tech-savvy job searching and to learn more about existing and emerging technologies in order to consider their usefulness and potential for clients. As has been the case with computer-assisted career guidance programs, these social networking sites are becoming more similar as time goes by. Many individuals have developed multiple public profiles. They have a website, a blog, and at least one social networking group to which they belong. Everything is connected to everything. A person's blog might become their website, or a person's website might include links to a person's blog and professional identity site, which in turn has a link to updated blog posts. Helping an individual best organize and manage these multiple technological outlets may be one of the most helpful interventions a career practitioner can offer.

References

Connell, R. S. (2009). Academic libraries, Facebook and MySpace, and student outreach: A survey of student opinion. *Libraries and the Academy, 9,* 25–36.

Kolek, E. A., & Saunders, D. (2008). Online disclosure: An empirical examination of undergraduate Facebook profiles. *NASPA Journal, 45,* 2–35.

Kluemper, D. H., & Rosen, P. A. (2009). Future employment selection methods: Evaluating social networking websites. *Journal of Managerial Psychology, 24,* 567–580.

Morris, J., Reese, J., Beck, R., & Mattis, C. (2010). Facebook usage as a predictor of retention at a private 4-year institution. *Journal of College Student Retention: Research, Theory & Practice, 11,* 311–322.

Roblyer, M. D., McDaniel, M., Webb, M., Herman, J., & Witty, J. V. (2010). Findings on Facebook in higher education: A comparison of college faculty and student uses and perceptions of social networking sites. *Internet and Higher Education, 13,* 134–140.

Steinfield, C., Ellison, N. B., & Lampe, C. (2008). Social capital, self-esteem, and use of online social network sites: A longitudinal analysis. *Journal of Applied Developmental Psychology, 29,* 434–445.

Chapter 5
ONLINE RESOURCES FOR CAREER DECISION MAKING

As a career practitioner, is it necessary to create a website, perhaps even adding an online career resource center for use by your clients or others? Jamie McKenzie (1997) argued that schools should create websites because (a) properly constructed websites become information systems that efficiently structure content to provide users with knowledge and insight, and (b) a good website helps people find worthwhile information with a minimum of wasted time. Since then, the expansive growth of the Internet and availability of resources for career and employment purposes makes his early arguments even more valid. Career practitioners should consider creating an online career resource center (OCRC) to guide clients in their use of the Internet as a career exploration and job search tool, providing a carefully selected collection of useful and usable resources that supports the work done in the counseling process.

There are several issues which must be addressed before, during, and after development of an online career resource center, specifically (a) design (visual as well as information structure), (b) selection of resources and services to be included, and (c) the continued maintenance and development of the entire website. There is a tremendous amount of overlap in these tasks, but each must be considered and addressed during the planning, implementation, and continued maintenance of the OCRC.

Designing the OCRC

The design process begins by determining the audience or target user group for this OCRC. Different users may require different designs as well as content. While it is likely a publicly-accessible OCRC will be used by persons who are not clients, this audience should not be considered part of the target user group. Only consider the clients actually served—students in a specific educational institution, users in a workforce development center, or clients in a private practice. Career practitioners who work with only one specific group will probably do best with a small yet highly-focused website where numerous resources targeted in one subject area can fill the list, while others who work with clients from varied socio-economic groups, occupations, and industries may need an OCRC with numerous subsections and different resource lists for each group.

Counselors who work with visually- or physically-impaired clients will need to consider issues of compatibility with the adaptive software programs used by these groups, and anyone working with persons unfamiliar with computers will find yet another set of design challenges to be met. If using outside developers to create a site, it is important to emphasize and argue for the needs of these clients in the visual design and navigation of the site. Practitioners should not sacrifice usability and usefulness for visual appeal and the latest technology.

Another issue that affects website design is purpose. Sites designed to market organizations and sell services are not the same as those designed as instructional guides. The site's purpose affects the organization of information and resources. It is possible to combine marketing and instruction in a single organizational website by dividing it into different categories such as Information for Employers, Potential Clients, Current Clients, etc., but the purpose of each category must be clearly defined with each area designed to match the specific purpose.

The OCRC should focus on instruction, not on marketing, which will help define a design structure. Sampson, Carr, Panke, Arkin, Minvielle, and Vernick (2003) discussed two options—resource-based designs and need-based designs—noting that a need-based approach to web design parallels the counseling process by identifying the client, determining his or her needs, and providing the resources and services necessary to meet those needs. Many website designers find this to be the most instructive way to present information to users as it creates a step-through process which can be followed to a great extent without the intervention of a practitioner. It is possible to structure the OCRC to require users to consider some topics and exercises before others, such as career exploration and job search process before an actual search of sites with job listings.

The design of the OCRC is also affected by its size, as well as its maintenance. How many subject areas are planned for inclusion, and how many links within each topic? The size of these areas affects the creation of the site and the selection of material for inclusion. The *NCDA Guidelines for the Use of the Internet for Provision of Career Information and Planning Services* (National Career Development Association, 2006) state that the professional who links to an external site is responsible for assuring that the external site also meets NCDA guidelines. To properly select content, it is important to review each site, service, or resource being considered. This process requires time to connect, read, consider, and document each decision. Reviewing a single link can take as little as 5 minutes or as much as 30 minutes depending on the quality of the site and the quantity of data found. For most practitioners, creating a smaller site means less time spent in content review and selection. Sampson (2008) also advocates limiting the number of links to external sites to lessen the possibility of overwhelming users with information, a major problem that must be considered in advocating the use of Internet-based resources. Following the concept that "smaller is better" simplifies the work of guiding users to high-quality resources and services, simplifies maintenance of the site, and offers room for growth as new, exemplary resources and services are discovered and considered for inclusion.

Selection of Resources and Services to be Included in the OCRC

Once the site design has been decided, it is possible to begin what is the most difficult part of the development process—the selection of resources. While deciding on the types of sites and resources to be added to the OCRC, it's important to establish a set of standards by which resources will be selected (Epstein & Lenz, 2008). Librarians refer to this as a collection development policy, and its primary function as defined by International Federation of Library Associations and Institutions (2001) is "... to provide guidance to staff when selecting and de-selecting (printed and electronic) resources for the local collection. [...] The main reason to write a collection development policy is to prevent the library from being driven by events or by individual enthusiasms and from purchasing a random set of resources, which may not support the mission of the library" (p. 2).

The policy serves not only as a guide for selecting sites and services to be included in the OCRC but it also governs the review of current content should the primary purpose of a selected resource change. It can also establish limits on the total number of external links to be maintained, including guidelines on determining what might be removed in order to make space for something new. At minimum, a collection development policy should include information on the types of resources that will be considered, specific pieces of data that must be present, and any criteria that may force a rejection of any resource. Length and detail is not as important as making sure the policy is an accurate statement of the professional and/or organizational intentions for the OCRC. Smaller organizations may find a simpler policy works well, something similar to the guidelines posted by *The Riley Guide* (2010). Larger organizations employing numerous career practitioners and assistants may need a formal document with detailed review processes and standards for documenting decisions. Epstein and Lenz (2008) discuss the outline and considerations for such a document and provide a sample policy. Additional collection development policies can be found online by performing a search on the phrase "collection development policy" in any search engine.

An important component of the collection development policy is the actual criteria used in evaluating the sites and services being considered for inclusion in the OCRC. The criteria themselves do not need to be explicitly stated in a public document, but they must be documented in some form, especially for organizations with more than one person handling resource selection. Despite disclaimers to the contrary, the presentation of a link on a site is considered an endorsement of that resource or service. To that end, it is important to think about NCDA's guidelines along with a personal consideration of any site, resource, or service, and judge each using professional as well as personal standards.

What sort of criteria might be used in evaluating a site, service, or resource for inclusion? Epstein and Lenz (2008) provide a very good sample evaluation form which can be adapted for use. Another set of criteria are those established by The Internet Scout Project (2010) for judging sites to be included in its weekly *Scout Report,* a free e-newsletter offering a selection of high-quality online resources of interest to researchers, educators, and others. This set of six criteria covers most major issues which should be considered in reviewing sites and resources for inclusion in the OCRC, and it can be easily expanded by the addition of specific questions to ask while considering sites and resources.

1. Content—what does this site offer, who is the intended audience, and is it accurate to the best of your knowledge? If it is a site offering job listings, does the database have a significant number of listings? Do those listings fit the stated mission of this site? What can be viewed without registering? Do you, the reviewer, agree with the information presented and the advice offered? Is this information copied from another source and merely reprinted here?

2. Authority—who is the author, and by what means may he or she claim authority in this area? Is there contact information for the owner/operator of the site beyond an e-mail form or the traditional "webmaster@XXX" e-mail address should assistance be required?

3. Information Maintenance—is the site current and updated on a regular basis? If the site offers a job database, are the jobs current (posted within the last week or month)? Are links to other sites active? If this site offers a job database, are listings older than 90, 120, 180 days deleted?

4. Presentation—how is the site organized, is it easy to navigate, is it easy to find the information needed? Will this site be accessible by persons who use assistive technologies to access the Internet? Does it require "helper" applications such as Flash, Java, PDF readers, or other software for full access? If the site offers online tools and/or assessments, must these be completed in a single sitting or can the user stop and return?

5. Availability—does the site respond? Do the pages within the site load quickly?

6. Cost—what is the full cost for access to a site that charges? What is the refund policy if someone is not satisfied with the services or products purchased? How is payment to be made?

Other criteria that may be considered as part of the review process include:

- Longevity—how long has this site been in existence? Does it have an established presence online?

- Open Access—how much of the site and its resources can be viewed without registering? If required, what does registering entail (e.g., significant personal information, a resume)?

- Privacy Policy—does this site protect the user's information? If the site is intended for children and young adults, is it specified how personal information is protected in relation to the Children's Online Privacy Protection Act (http://business.ftc.gov/documents/bus45-how-comply-childrens-online-privacy-protection-rule)

- Discovery—how was this site found? Was it recommended by a colleague who has used it? Was it found through another trusted source? Was it a reciprocal link exchange request?

The issue of reciprocal link exchanges is one to be addressed in the collection development policy. A public website with links to external sources will receive these requests, usually phrased as "if you will link to us, we will link back to you." An entire business called Search Engine Optimization (SEO) has been built around this exercise because search engines like Google are thought to rank search results based on popularity—the more sites that link to a certain site, the better it must be.

This ignores the second ranking algorithm used by the same search engines, namely relevance. Google Webmaster Central (2010) includes the following statement on Link Schemes: "The quantity, quality, and relevance of links count towards your rating. The sites that link to you can provide context about the subject matter of your site, and can indicate its quality and popularity" (para. 1). It may not be necessary to include a formal statement on reciprocal links in the collection development policy, but it is better to refuse to participate and instead offer to evaluate submissions based on their relevance to this select list of site and services. Be aware that if hiring an outside developer to create and market a website, it will be necessary to ask about the marketing campaign to ensure that the quality of the site and its relevance will not be affected.

The most important thing to remember when reviewing any online site, service, or resource for inclusion in an OCRC is that the developer of the site is the best judge of what is to be included. Personal reactions to what is being viewed are important. Be critical and be selective. Is this site, service, or resource really good enough to recommend it to others? There are more than enough sites to fill the needs of clients and more than enough large directories of online career and employment information. Clients want guidance in the selection and use of these resources. The best rating system available is personal, professional judgment. Judge each online site, service, and resource as if it was a new service, resource, or tool being considered for personal use or for use in personal practice.

Maintenance of the OCRC

What is involved in maintenance, and why is this an issue? At its most basic level it is link checking, verifying on a regular basis that the links on the OCRC site pointing to external sites and/or resources are still "live" or accessible. Links change, or even break, for many reasons. A website owner may redesign his or her site, moving pages to new areas. A page may be deleted because it is no longer relevant to that site. The new owner of an existing site may decide to alter the way content is archived online. A website may have merged with another site and the old domain name is now "redirected" to the new site. Even the simple process of changing the software used to deliver page content can affect links. Whatever the reason for the change, the result of a nonfunctioning or "broken" link is the same: the user cannot find the page sought, which could translate into a frustrated client, a refusal to use these resources, and an unprofessional impression of services provided.

Link checking can be automated to a degree by using link-checking software and services such as LinkAlarm.com and NetMechanic.com, but these can only check active links and report problems or changes. These robot services cannot review the content of the sites, leaving the practitioner to review and revisit links on a regular basis. Like businesses, websites are bought, sold, and consolidated. Domain names are also traded in the same way, meaning the link may be the same but the content and mission of the site may have changed drastically to the point that it no longer fits in the OCRC. These changes will only become apparent during a live review; fewer links to external sources will simplify this time-consuming process.

Internet Sites for Career Planning

The items in the following list include many resources, services, and tools which assist users in exploring careers, planning for the future, searching for employment, and finding the additional training necessary to pursue a dream. Most of these resources are free, and several were developed in countries other than the United States. This is a mere sample of what is available online, but it can serve as a starting point for a new collection or help to expand an older one.

Directories of Online Employment and Career Guides

These guides offer listings of employment resources, career exploration guides, salary guides, and much more. These are useful for searching for resources not included here and for additional services to fit the needs of specific clients.

job-hunt.org. One of the earliest guides to the Internet job search, Job-Hunt.org offers numerous carefully selected links to job search resources for the world. Users can search for job sites by location, profession, industry, or job type. The site owner, Susan Joyce, also has included other useful articles, information resources, and articles on protecting privacy online and choosing a job site.

jobhuntersbible.com. This online guide to the job search is developed and maintained by Richard Bolles. It was developed to supplement his print publications and is spiced with his comments and observations on the job search and the decision-making process. Included on this site is his Net Guide to the best job search and career information sites online.

rileyguide.com. The Riley Guide: Employment Opportunities and Job Resources on the Internet has the distinction of being the first guide to the Internet as a tool for finding new employment. Margaret Riley Dikel started this site in January 1994 and continues to maintain it as a free resource. The Riley Guide links to hundreds of sources of information for job leads, career exploration, and potential employers. It has information to help users find the best ways to use the Internet in their job search, explore new careers, research new places to live, and consider education and training options.

Self-Assessment

Many well-known, validated inventories are currently available online from their publishers. We have not included those tools here and invite readers to see *A Counselor's Guide to*

Career Assessment Instruments, Fifth Edition (Whitfield, Feller, & Wood, 2009) for information. This short list of primarily free resources includes tools suitable for youth, young adults, and older clients, but it is necessary for the practitioner to review each for suitability and usability for OCRC clientele.

assessment.com. Motivational Assessment of Personal Potential (MAPP) is an interest survey designed by the International Assessment Network in Minneapolis, MN. A free sample MAPP Career Analysis is provided to help individuals identify their preferences for working with people or things, and other job characteristics; it also suggests some occupations that match these preferences. The assessment takes about 20 minutes to complete, but it is possible to stop the inventory and resume it at a later time. The resulting report is sent to the user via e-mail, outlining his or her "natural motivations and talent for work" and matching these to five occupational descriptions from O*NET. MAPP offers varied access points for individuals, students (including K–12), corporate users, workforce development offices, and career coaches. MAPP is available in 6 languages: English, French, Polish, Portuguese, Spanish, and Swedish.

queendom.com. Queendom offers a variety of personality, intelligence, and health tests and quizzes. These offer a full range of professional-quality, scientifically-validated psychological assessments designed to allow users to reach their potential through feedback and custom-tailored analysis. The site is a subsidiary of PsychTests AIM Inc., a high-tech psychometric company that develops a suite of products and services centered on its extensive battery of psychological assessments. Information on their development and validation is available under "About the Site." All users can register for free and take a short form of most of these assessments and tests at no cost, but some tests as well as extended personalized result reports will cost some fee.

https://emanual.uwaterloo.ca/. The first section of the award-winning *Career Development eManual* from the University of Waterloo Career Services is a collection of six assessment exercises complete with information about what each is intended to accomplish, forms and/or exercises which may be printed out and completed. The assessment process finishes by integrating all that has been learned and/or discovered into a neat package which will help guide the user through the remainder of his or her career development process. These assessments cover personality and attitude, skills and achievements, knowledge and learning style, values, interests (based on Holland's theory), and entrepreneurism. Individuals outside of the University of Waterloo community are charged a fee for access which is good for 90 days. Institutions are welcome to inquire about group discounts.

cddq.org. The Career Decision-Making Difficulties Questionnaire (CDDQ) is based on research performed at the Hebrew University of Jerusalem and The Ohio State University by a team led by Professors Itamar Gati and Samuel H. Osipow. This site includes five assessments designed to assist individuals in the process of making a career decision by helping them clarify what their specific difficulties are, by providing a framework for a systematic process for career decision making organized into a three-stage process, and by providing the career professional with information about and access to Making Better Career Decisions (MBCD), an Internet-based career planning system. All of the assessments are free to use, and the supporting documentation is available for perusal.

caseylifeskills.org. Casey Life Skills, the Ansell-Casey Life Skills Assessments (ASCLA), are a set of free and simple-to-use tools designed to evaluate the life skills of youths and young adults with the goal of helping young people prepare for adulthood. The assessments are completed online and provide instant feedback. A variety of learning plans provide a clear outline of next steps, and the accompanying teaching resources are available for free or at a minimal cost. This suite of comprehensive online assessments, learning plans, and learning resources was designed to engage young people in foster care, aiding them in developing the life skills needed to exit care, but any practitioner who works with children and young adults in less than ideal situations or even recent immigrants will find these extremely useful. The various assessments are targeted to different development ages from 8 to 18 years and up and are available in English, Spanish, and French. It is not necessary to have an e-mail address to use them, and the Organization ID and Youth ID are for clients and practitioners only. Much more information is provided in the Frequently Asked Questions.

http://www.iseek.org/careers/skillsAssessment. The iSeek Skills Assessment is based on data from O*NET and is a fairly simple tool that allows the user to rate him or herself on 35 different skills and then see what occupations match those skills identified as the being most important to the user. The entire tool takes 5–10 minutes to complete, and the results are presented immediately upon completion, offering the user information on each career, how his or her skills match this profile, and the level of education or training usually required to perform this particular job. The user interface is relatively simple and should not pose a problem for persons with limited computer skills. Individuals can print the results page, e-mail it to a career practitioner or other person, or save the results to a free iSeek account.

Career Development Process

These resources offer guidance through the entire career planning and exploration process and address the needs of different populations and age groups.

iseek.org. iSeek, Minnesota's Career, Education, and Job Resource, is a simple guide that helps users of all types answer the question of "What do you seek?" by covering career exploration, education planning, and job search in a single source. Sponsored by iSeek Solutions, a Minnesota partnership formed in 1999 to work with the state's workforce development and education authorities to develop and inform policy and to strategize services, this site allows users to decide where to start and how to progress. The ultimate goal is the help the user create a career development plan, including instructions on how to implement it. Users can register for free accounts in order to customize their personal interests and receive updates. One nice feature appears at the bottom of the front page where information guides for specific users (e.g., recent immigrants, ex-offenders, veterans, the disabled) are provided. The Reality Check is a great way to get young adults thinking about expenses after graduation.

kuderjourney.com. The Kuder Journey was developed by Kuder specifically for postsecondary schools and adult career changers. Kuder Journey is a career guidance product designed to guide these older and often more experienced users through the process of planning for a career, making a career change, or merely making sure a career is still on track. The goal is to not only lead someone to a career but also consider the management of the personal process we call a career. As users complete their initial registration, the system asks about needs, personal situation, and potential barriers to career and employment, and also asks for the user to identify his or her user type, including career changer, veteran or active-duty military, disabled adult, ex-offender, or retiree. The inclusion of these specific user types makes this a valuable product for many career counseling or support situations and service providers. Site licensing is available to practitioners, or users can purchase individual access.

http://careerresource.coedu.usf.edu/Index.html. The Career Resources Page was developed by two professors in the counselor education program at the University of South Florida. The purpose of this free webpage is to provide information about Internet resources to students and individuals interested in developing a career plan and exploring career options. The website houses many links on self-assessment, general and specific career searches, career information, and job preparation. In addition, there are lists of tools for students, career specialists, and individuals interested in career resources, such as example card sorts, a career laboratory, and an interactive career laboratory that houses the Virtual Card Sort.

https://emanual.uwaterloo.ca/. The University of Waterloo's Career Services Center developed the Career Development eManual, a six-step process to aid users in career and life-planning. Starting with self-assessment and working through research, decision making, networks and contacts, work, and life/work planning, users review articles under each area and work through various exercises designed to help them not only find a job but also develop and maintain a satisfying career. Individuals outside of the University of Waterloo community are charged a fee for access which is good for 90 days. Institutions are welcome to inquire about group discounts.

Occupational Information

These various occupational guides offer career profiles in different formats and for different audiences. Many are government publications, not just the U.S Government, but each offers interesting information and all are free.

careerinfonet.org. America's Career InfoNet is part of CareerOneStop and offers visitors a variety of tools and resources for career exploration, education information, and even job search instruction. Its purpose is to help users explore career opportunities and make informed employment and education choices. The site features user-friendly occupation and industry information, salary data, career videos, education resources, self-assessment tools, career exploration assistance, and other resources that support career exploration and development in today's marketplace. Specific sections offer information and resources targeted to transitioning military personnel and auto workers downsized in the current economic market, as well as additional resources for out-of-work individuals.

bls.gov/oco/cg/. The *Career Guide to Industries* provides information on currently available careers sorted by industry. Each description includes the nature of the industry, working conditions, employment, occupations in the industry, training and advancement, earnings and benefits, employment outlook, and lists of organizations that can provide additional information. It is a way to find out who is needed by various industries and assess a lateral move from one industry to another. Like the *Occupational Outlook Handbook* and the *Occupational Outlook Quarterly*, this guide comes from the U.S. Bureau of Labor Statistics and is free.

myfuture.edu.au. Myfuture is a joint product of Australian, state, and territory governments and a wonderful career and occupational guide. Individual users can register for a free account which allows them to customize the site and save information while exploring occupations and planning careers, but users can also review the facts of this site, browsing information on careers, work and employment, education and training, funding, and support services. Under the heading of "Assist Others" are resources to help groups like parents or teachers help children and adolescents with career planning. Some of the resources used to develop this site are based on similar products in O*Net, but the occupation and industry data is specific to Australia and New Zealand.

bls.gov/oco/. The *Occupational Outlook Handbook* (OOH) is one of the most quoted and cited career information guides available. It is a career reference that describes the job duties, working conditions, education and training requirements, earnings levels, current employment levels, projected employment change, and employment prospects for hundreds of occupations. It presents the results of research and analysis conducted by the Bureau of Labor Statistics' Office of Occupational Statistics and Employment Projections to help students and job seekers identify and learn about careers. Users can search the handbook using keywords, browse occupational families using the links and menus on the left, or scan the A–Z index for ideas.

Each profile also includes a list of related occupations and sources for additional information, usually professional or trade associations and other quality related organizations. Each profile can be easily printed in PDF format by clicking on the link at the top of each page. The guide is updated every two years, and a Spanish version with a slightly smaller occupation list is available. This version of the OOH is intended for upper-level students and adults (educators and school counselors will want to look at the Teacher's Guide, found in the left menu). Those who work with grades 4–8 will appreciate the simpler version of the OOH, the BLS kids' page (bls.gov/k12/), accompanied by a second teacher's guide. All of the various online versions of this product are free.

bls.gov/opub/ooq/. The *Occupational Outlook Quarterly* (OOQ) is published quarterly by the Bureau of Labor Statistics. This print and online magazine features articles with practical information on jobs and careers. It covers a wide variety of career and work-related topics, such as new and emerging occupations, training opportunities, salary trends, and results of new studies from the Bureau of Labor Statistics. Articles are usually presented in PDF format and require the appropriate software for viewing and printing (the free Adobe Reader is one example). Some articles are also published in HTML format as well as PDF, and can be read quickly online or printed for future reading. Past articles are also accessible by selecting either the topic-oriented index or the individual issue archive from the left menu. Two columns of particular note are "You're a what?," profiling a different unusual occupation in each issue, and "The Grab Bag," featuring news tips for practitioners as well as clients. This publication is free online with a paper subscription available for a nominal fee.

online.onetcenter.org. O*NET OnLine was created to provide broad access to the O*NET (Occupational Information Network) database of occupational information, which includes information on skills, abilities, work activities, and interests associated with over 950 occupations. This user-friendly resource allows visitors to browse occupations by career cluster, industry, job family, job zone (level of education usually required), or other current interests such as green economy or STEM (science / technology / engineering / math) discipline. Users can also search for possible careers by skills or tools and technology needed. Some users will also appreciate the crosswalks, allowing them to match careers and jobs to Military Occupational Classifications (MOC), apprenticeship codes, or titles from the Registered Apprenticeship Partners Information Data System (RAPIDS) or other systems. Occupational information is gathered primarily from related BLS sources such as the *Occupational Outlook Handbook,* but a particularly nice feature within these reports is the inclusion of data such as the three-part Holland code, national employment and wage data which can be narrowed down to a specific state, and related occupations which are flagged for green jobs and those with particularly "Bright Outlooks" for growth. These make for extremely detailed occupational reports, but their accessibility and readability makes the entire system a pleasure for users as well as practitioners and educators.

vaview.org. Virginia Career VIEW (Vital Information for Education and Work) is a source for career and education information in the Commonwealth of Virginia with sections focused on students (divided by grade/age), parents, and professionals. Career explorers can quickly find information on various careers either by Career Cluster or by selecting a specific career that interests them. Students in younger grades will find numerous age-appropriate tools and resources for them. Parents will find helpful guides and tools to work with their children in examining career options. Professionals will find guides, links to associations and training, and even more resources to help them guide their clients and students in their efforts. While the occupational data and primary education information is linked to Virginia, most users will find this to be a terrific source of information and guidance.

Employment Trends

Employment data encompasses not only what occupations are growing but also where the jobs are, meaning the city, county, or state. Labor market information compiled by the states is the best source of these data, but it can be difficult to understand. Practitioners should review the data from these resources before referring clients to sites in order to guide them to the data needed to make an informed decision. The resources listed under Occupational Information, above, will have some information on employment trends.

rileyguide.com/trends.html#gov. The Riley Guide includes state-level labor market information on employment, wages, industries, and other factors affecting the world of work. The problem is that most of the data reported in the news is aggregated at a national level (the Bureau of Labor Statistics) and may not apply to your specific state or city. This collection of links from The Riley Guide takes users to labor market information for the individual states to locate much more relevant data.

bls.gov/emp/ep_data_occupational_data.htm. Occupational data from the U.S. Bureau of Labor Statistics presents a specific page of tables, analyses, articles, and more will give users their most accessible and understandable view of occupational employment projections from 2008 to 2018 as well as the ability to review current and projected earnings for the same period. At the very top of the page is a short selection of the most popular data charts showing the fastest growing occupations along with those expected to experience the largest employment growth. Scroll down the page to view projected earnings data at a national, state, or metropolitan level and then use their guided search tool to compare employment, training, and earnings data for a variety of occupations based on either the education and training level necessary or the occupation selected. BLS has an overwhelming amount of data which can be confusing to most users who attempt to view it on their own. This particular selection of tables and tools can provide a significant snapshot of possible growth areas in a relatively easy-to-understand form and formula.

Salary Information

Salary data can help users determine possible future earnings from a potential career or establish a beginning point for compensation negotiations with a potential employer. These large sites offer job and industry-specific data along with some specific location variation. In addition, many sites listed within the Resources for Specific Industries and Occupations (below) will have salary data for the careers represented.

careeronestop.org/SalariesBenefits/SalariesBenefits.aspx. All users will appreciate the easy-to-find and easy-to-understand wage and salary information found at CareerOneStop.org: Salaries and Benefits Information under the Wages and Salaries title. Try the "For Occupations" search to quickly find national-level wage data for hundreds of occupations, data which can then be focused on a specific state or metropolitan region. It is possible to search for these same data starting with a specific location by selecting either By Location or Compare Metro Wages. All of the wage data is provided by the Occupational Employment Statistics program of the U.S. Bureau of Labor Statistics, but most users will find this a much more friendly form. Other sections included in this part of CareerOneStop include discussions of Relocation, Unemployment Insurance, Pay for Education & Training (with a very nice article on how earnings improves with education), and Benefits.

jobstar.org/tools/salary/. JobStar has put together what many consider to be the most comprehensive collection of salary surveys online. Combined with lists of books to request from local libraries and articles from experts such as Jack Chapman, this site provides users with excellent guidance for salary research.

bls.gov/oes/. The Occupational Employment Statistics (OES) program produces employment and wage estimates for more than 800 occupations. These are estimates of the number of people employed in certain occupations, and estimates of the wages paid to them. Self-employed persons are not included in the estimates. These estimates are available for the nation as a whole, for individual states, and for metropolitan areas; national occupational estimates for specific industries are also available. As with much of the data produced by BLS, the various reports and datasets can be overwhelming for many users. Practitioners can start with the OES Tables as these will present the most relevant data in the most readable fashion. Then if more detail is preferred, users can go to the full database to create a customized report. The article "How Jobseekers and Employers Can Use Occupational Employment Statistics (OES) Data during Wage and Salary Discussions" (bls.gov/oes/highlight_wage_discussions.htm) offers an excellent discussion of how location and even industry affects earnings and relevant discussions with employers.

salary.com. This site offers users free access to more than just salary data. Salary.com gives users information on total compensation, not only what is in the paycheck but also the benefits and perquisites received on the job. The Salary Wizard allows users to search for base, median, and top-level earnings in hundreds of jobs in many occupational areas; many of these projections are local as well as national. Users will have to register for a free account in order to complete and view the survey, but it is still a much less complicated and involved process than some of the other free salary reports. Salary.com uses a team of compensation specialists to add value to salary surveys done by others, such as the Bureau of Labor Statistics. Users will find helpful articles and exercises on figuring things like benefits, stock options, bonuses (and how to get them), and salary negotiations.

For a very reasonable fee, users can buy a Personal Salary Report, a very detailed examination of their earning power based on their personal work history and geographic location. Other good free tools for users include the two Cost of Living tools found in the "Personal" area of the site. The first is the Cost of Living Wizard included in the Statistics Center. This allows someone to easily find relevant cost of living data for his or her current location and compare this to other parts of the country. The second is the Cost of Living Calculator found at the bottom of the page. A user can quickly enter a base salary, current living and working locations, and targeted locations to see what salary adjustments may be necessary in order to maintain a certain standard of living. These do not require registration to view.

Educational Information

These free directories and databases include listings for colleges, distance education programs, vocational training, and short-term training programs that range from one day to two years. Many also include information on funding for education and training programs.

careeronestop.org/EducationTraining/Find/Short-TermTraining.aspx. CareerOneStop: Short-Term Training Finder is a free searchable directory that lists training programs ranging from less than a year up to two years in length. These can be either preparation courses for certification exams or instruction programs leading to issuance of a certification upon completion. The directory can be searched by occupation, school, program, or keywords describing the program or certification desired. It can then be customized by length of program (more or less than one year), and location (state or a specific distance from a particular zip code). The search results will list institutions matching the search specifications, and each listing will provide the user with brief information on institution, including contact information and a website (if available). It will also link the user to related certifications and other relevant career information for the particular program sought. Each listing's report can be saved as a Word document for printing and later referral.

careeronestop.org/TRAINING/TrainingEduHome.asp. The CareerOneStop: Training and Education Center is a free resource for information on degree programs, specialty training opportunities, financial aid, certification and accreditation, and licensing for the various states. It also includes career information and links it to education and training plans. There are links to additional training and education information and articles on how to ensure the quality of the training before signing up for a program. The Training and Education Center is part of America's Career Infonet, a subsection of CareerOneStop. To find it from the front page, select America's Career Infonet from the More Resources tab in the upper-right part of the front page.

nces.ed.gov/collegenavigator/. College Navigator is a research tool that allows access to information on more than 9,000 colleges, universities, and postsecondary vocational and technical schools in the U.S. Users may search the database by location, type of institution, program and majors offered, availability of housing, and many more options. Users have the option of selecting several school profiles for side-by-side comparisons, and all search results can be sent to a valid e-mail address, printed, or exported as an Excel spreadsheet. The site and all of its information is also available in Spanish. This is a product of the National Center for Education Statistics (NCES), part of the U.S. Department of Education's Institute of Education Sciences.

detc.org. The Distance Education and Training Council (DETC) is a nonprofit educational association that sponsors a nationally recognized accrediting agency for distance education programs. Users visiting the website can find a searchable directory of accredited high school and college degree programs, including some offered by federal and military schools. There is also a list of general areas of study offered through the accredited programs, with specific course and institutional information under each. Practitioners and educators will also want to make their clients and students aware of some of the free publications available from DETC, including their pamphlets titled "Is Distance Education for You?" and "Don't Take No For An Answer," which will guide a student working to transfer distance credits to a new program. Most documents are in PDF format and will require the free Adobe reader or other similar software for viewing and printing.

gocollege.com. GoCollege is a free searchable guide with information on how to finance and succeed in college. Visitors can review information on admissions (selecting schools, test preparation, application essays, and more), financial aid (loans, scholarships, and grants), education options (types of schools and varieties of programs), and college survival (money maintenance, study tips, and dealing with dorm life). GoCollege has searchable databases for financial aid as well as information on and links to loan providers. There is a lot of information here to guide potential students, including older students who are considering a return to school or the pursuit of additional degrees or certifications.

petersons.com. Peterson's, the well-known publisher of guides to colleges, provides this free searchable resource for information on a variety of training and education programs, including undergraduate and graduate programs, professional schools, and distance education programs. Among the many descriptions of institutions and degree possibilities are articles on applying for college (both undergraduate and graduate), selecting a school and a program, and much more. Within the Undergraduate section is a financial-aid search system which requires registration along with numerous practice programs for the many standardized tests an individual may encounter (fee). Persons interested in graduate school will find helpful articles on ways to finance these studies, including discussions on fellowships, grants, and teaching assistant programs. All users can scroll to the bottom of almost every page to find quick-links to popular topics of interest, such as Late Deadline Schools, Study Abroad, and Historically Black Colleges.

rwm.org. The RWM Vocational School Database includes private postsecondary vocational-technical schools in all 50 states, organized by state and the training programs offered. This list includes private schools that offer certificates, diplomas, associate (junior college) degrees, and bachelor (college) degrees in various business, trade, and technical disciplines as well as online programs. All the schools listed are state approved or accredited, but the information is limited to the institution's name, address, and phone number. At the top of each state is a link to resources for that state from the U.S. Department of Education. Visually impaired users who would like to review the directory by state will need to use the first link on the word "state" in the introductory description or gain access through the Site Map at the bottom of the page. Under each heading there is a list of programs. Some offer links to their webpage and complete address information or even forms users may complete to request information from the school. Nonlinked listings indicate nonsubscriber schools, and the contact information for these may not be up-to-date. This directory is currently owned and operated by QuinStreet Inc., a vertical marketing and online media company.

seminarinformation.com. Originally founded in 1981 and turned into an online resource in 1999, SeminarInformation.com lists over 360,000 seminars and conferences hosted by associations, private organizations, and universities. Users of this free site can use the Quick Search to find upcoming programs by keywords from the title or description, browse the category lists to see what is offered in any given area, or target upcoming programs by location. Each listing includes a full description of the training program offered, the host, the location, and the cost. Users can register immediately through the page or print the training brochure for later referral.

usnews.com/sections/education/. The publisher of *U.S. News and World Report* has consistently produced one of the most outstanding guides to education information on the web. Dedicated sections of this area of the website focus on college, community college, graduate school, e-learning, and financial aid, and each is filled with quality news, information, and resources. USNews.com also lists the annual rankings of colleges and graduate schools.

Financial Aid Information

While many of the education and training guides listed above include information on financial aid, the following free sites focus on this information and may include searchable directories of scholarships and other funding programs.

www1.salliemae.com/before_college/. Sallie Mae has helped thousands achieve their dreams of higher education by providing funds for educational loans, primarily federally guaranteed student loans originated under the Federal Family Education Loan Program (FFELP). This free site allows students and parents to learn about many ways to pay for college, guides them through loan applications, and aids in managing their debt afterwards. The main SallieMae.com site also links to information on 529 savings plans along with other savings and loan programs offered by this particular lender.

finaid.org. Established in 1994, FinAid is possibly the finest single source for information and resources for all types of educational financial aid including military aid programs and prepaid tuition/529 savings plans. Under each category visitors will find comprehensive information on various programs, advice on how to approach each, important legislative information, warnings about potential problems or even scams, and much more. There are numerous calculators to help students and parents figure out how much is needed, the true cost of a loan, and almost anything else a user could dare to ask. Educators are also included with guides to help them work with students and parents. This continues to be the premiere site for financial aid information online, and it continues to be free.

studentaid.ed.gov. This site is a one-stop center for all of the U.S. Department of Education's Federal Student Aid (FSA) programs. Available in English and Spanish, this site will guide the user through the process of preparing for college, selecting and applying to schools, securing funding from a variety of sources, attending college, and repaying loans. Information is available for high school, undergraduate, and graduate students as well as parents, international students, and other targeted student populations. The site links to FAFSA, the Free Application for Federal Student Aid (fafsa.ed.gov) for easy access and application processing. A few portions of the site require the user to create a login and password, but this is to allow the users to save profile information, store applications, and customize areas for specific needs. Users can review their extensive privacy policy from the link at the bottom of each page for information on how this data is used and protected. Under Tools and Resources are links to additional funding resources, including StudentLoans.gov, the National Student Loan Data System (NSLDS), and more.

Apprenticeships and Other Alternative Training Programs

These programs offer the opportunity to learn a new trade or gain experience in a particular filed outside of a traditional college-level education program. Some are volunteer positions requiring a minimum commitment and offering other benefits in return. All are worth exploring and are not limited to young adults.

apprenticesearch.com/fpTrades/trades.asp. This Canadian site for employers and apprentices, About Trades from Apprenticesearch.com, includes a list of trades that have apprenticeships. In addition to information on wages, prospects, and working conditions, each trade includes a small self-assessment to determine if the trade would be a good fit. It's a great way for job seekers to begin researching skilled trades. Non-Canadian users will find valuable information here, but should then switch to a relevant local site for wage and specific training requirements like the *Occupational Outlook Handbook* (bls.gov/ooh) for the United States.

careeronestop.org/EducationTraining/Find/Certification.aspx. Certifications are examinations that test or enhance your knowledge, experience, or skills in an occupation or profession. This directory from CareerOneStop allows users to search for certifications by keyword, industry, or occupation. Certifications are generally voluntary but may be required by some employers in some occupations. In some cases, there are additional certifications that licensed individuals may want to pursue in order to advance into a new specialty, but in other cases these are more useful for demonstrating a specific skill or a continued improvement in skills which are applicable to your current employment situation.

nationalservice.gov. Established in 1993, the Corporation for National and Community Service oversees programs engaging more than a million Americans each year in service to their communities. The Corporation's three major service initiatives are AmeriCorps, Learn and Serve America, and the Senior Corps, but it also supports other initiatives such as the Martin Luther King, Jr. Day of Service. The AmeriCorps program provides credits and/or awards to assist with the payment of education costs or loans.

clearhq.org. The Council on Licensure, Enforcement, and Regulation (CLEAR) international organization serves those entities or individuals involved in the licensure, nonvoluntary certification, or registration of the hundreds of regulated occupations and professions. Individuals will appreciate the extensive links to these many organizations under the Regulatory Directory link in the left margin. These are divided by geographic region (North America, Europe, and Australasia), and the *North American Directory of Regulatory Boards and Colleges* can be browsed by profession or jurisdiction.

jobcorps.gov. Job Corps is the nation's largest residential education and training program for disadvantaged youth between the ages of 16 and 24. The Job Corps operates more than 100 centers around the country and in Puerto Rico, with a focus on training the whole person. General information on the program is available here, but more specific information along with a parents' guide is available on their recruiting website (recruiting.jobcorps.gov). Please note that U.S. citizenship is required to apply for this program.

peacecorps.gov. Founded in 1961 by President John F. Kennedy, the Peace Corps was established to promote world peace and friendship. This site contains background information on the organization, recruiting, diversity, and reach of this volunteer service program. It is developed for audiences of various ages, including information for teens who might consider this program in the future.

How to Find Registered Apprenticeship Programs

Registered Apprenticeship programs have trained millions of qualified individuals for lifelong careers since 1937. These programs provide structured, on-the-job learning for more than 1,000 career areas in traditional industries such as construction and manufacturing, as well as new emerging industries such as health care, information technology, energy, telecommunications, and more. The Federal Office of Apprenticeship within the United States Employment and Training Administration has a presence in almost all 50 states plus many territories, and interested persons can contact the relevant state or responsible regional office for information on programs available in his or her state of residence.

www.doleta.gov/oa/regdirlist.cfm. Regional Offices of Apprenticeship

www.doleta.gov/OA/stateoffices.cfm. State Offices of Apprenticeship

Many states offer their own registered apprenticeship programs, with much more specific information and documents for interested individuals.

www.doleta.gov/OA/sainformation.cfm. State Apprenticeship Agencies

www.doleta.gov/oa/stateagencies.cfm. Contact information for the State Apprenticeship Agencies

It is also possible to search the Office of Apprenticeship Sponsors website for a list of apprenticeship program sponsors recognized and registered by the Office of Apprenticeship or a State Registration Agency (oa.doleta.gov/eta_default.cfm). A search result will display the official name of the program sponsor along with street address, city, and state. The database does not indicate if the program is currently accepting applicants, but is a good way for individuals to begin a search. Finally, search engines such as Google (google.com) and Bing (bing.com) can also be used to find programs by searching on the words "apprentice," "apprenticeship," or "registered apprenticeship" plus additional terms describing the program that interests the user, such as "sheet metal" or "metalworker," or the state of residence.

Job Search Instruction and Advice

Practically everyone online is a master at job search and is more than willing to offer his or her advice on how to find work. This particular list of resources is limited to persons or groups who are acknowledged experts in their fields. This list also includes resources for those who are unfamiliar with computer and the Internet, for those searching for employment outside of the United States (or persons from outside the United States hoping to work here).

careermanagementalliance.com/blog. The Career Management Alliance is a professional association of career practitioners who provide services of all kinds to individuals seeking to advance their careers. While the website will link job seekers to the many career professionals who are members of this association, the combined articles from member blogs is a highly prized collection of job search and career advice.

goinglobal.com. GoinGlobal is a provider of both country-specific and USA city-specific career and employment information. Their e-books are researched by in-country career experts and updated annually to include information such as application and interviewing customs, employment trends, work permit and visa regulations, major employers, and much more. The individual guides are available to all for a moderate fee, and anyone working with international candidates, trailing spouses, or clients interested in exploring international possibilities will find these to be extremely useful.

jobhuntersbible.com. This guide from author Richard Bolles incorporates a megalist of online job resources with many of the self-assessment exercises and job searching hints from his print publications. Dick Bolles continues to be one of the best authorities available for both job seekers and those who aid them in their search.

jobweb.com. JobWeb from the National Association of Colleges and Employers (NACE) features information and articles to help college students with all aspects of the job search. Most of the articles and resources are targeted to the new college graduate, but many apply to users at other experience levels. Information for parents who are assisting recent or soon-to-graduate children in their search is also included.

susanireland.com. Susan Ireland's Resume Site is much more than the title indicates. This site includes extensive information on resume preparation, job search correspondence (it's more than just cover letters), and even interviewing. There are also terrific samples for users to review and use as templates for their own documents. Susan apprenticed under the late resume writer Yana Parker, and then trained others who are now members of her resume team. Susan has authored resume and cover letter writing software and four books on resume writing, cover letter writing, and job searching, and has appeared on radio, TV, and the Internet to discuss effective job search tools. The site is also available in Spanish. Users and counselors or coaches will appreciate Susan's blog, The Job Lounge (joblounge.blogspot.com).

www.rileyguide.com/kiosk.html. This page of the Riley Guide links to several free resources and services practitioners that clients can use to develop a familiarity with application kiosks and online job applications and even develop a printed application to be carried along to assist in submitting applications through in-house electronic stations. This is part of The Riley Guide's collection of articles on How to Job Search (rileyguide.com/execute.html).

wendyenelow.com. Wendy Enelow is a Master Resume Writer (MRW), Credentialed Career Manager (CCM), Certified Professional Resume Writer (CPRW), and a Certified Job and Career Transition Coach (JCTC), who has combined all of that plus a career of more than 20 years into this source for both job seekers and career professionals. Two different libraries of articles are shown under "Articles," and the collection for the Executive Job Seeker is actually useful for job seekers at all levels of experience and even includes some guidance for separating military personnel. The articles for Career Practitioners offer advice in preparing resumes for clients as well as business advice for practitioners.

online.wsj.com/public/page/news-career-jobs.html. The Wall Street Journal: Careers site continues to offer articles and information covering all aspects of the job search and career management. In this new format, content is being updated daily but the archiving of articles is not as extensive. Various new subsections cover new topics including Reinvent (career changes, etc.), Career Strategies, The Juggle (work/life balance), and numerous How-To Guides.

Job Banks

Large, general job banks are where most job seekers focus their time and effort in an online search. While there is some value to these services, these sites get far too much attention for the minimal return offered most job seekers. This particular list includes sites for college students and part-time or hourly positions.

careerbuilder.com. CareerBuilder is one of the larger and more dynamic sites for job and career information. Registration is free of charge and allows a job seeker to store a resume online without posting it in the database. Registered users can create up to five personal search profiles to track new jobs added to the database, and an e-mail message can be generated to a user when a match is discovered.

collegegrad.com. The College Grad Job Hunter website is a cornucopia of resources and information to guide college students and others through a complete job search. It has job databases for those seeking internships, entry-level job seekers, and experienced job seekers as well as a searchable database of more than 8,000 employers. It also offers advice on careers, the job search, resume preparation, and more.

groovejob.com. GrooveJob specializes in seasonal, part-time, and hourly jobs along with jobs for teens and students. Users can easily target jobs in their location by city/state or zip code to find possibilities with specific employers within 15 miles. Users must complete the free registration which includes a resume in order to apply for any listings found here.

jobcentral.com. JobCentral is operated by the Direct Employers Association, a nonprofit consortium of leading U.S. corporations, in alliance with the National Association of State Workforce Agencies. This association was established in 2001 by a consortium of employers who wanted to increase recruiting efficiency while reducing costs. Users will find numerous postings placed here by employers, with links leading back to employer websites for application purposes. JobCentral operates several targeted sites for diversity candidates, the disabled, veterans, and many more, and partners with several groups to provide effective recruiting and access to extensive opportunities.

monster.com. Monster.com is one of the most recognized names in the online job search industry. It offers an impressive variety of job and career resources for everyone from college students to contractors to chief executives; most are served with their own communities that include job listings and career advice. It also offers several industry/job field communities, including healthcare, human resources, and finance.

nationjob.com. NationJob features an impressive collection of job openings, company information, and a variety of ways to search the database. It divides into many sources of occupation- and/or industry-related resources, creating an excellent source of information for all. Users can easily search for jobs by keyword and location or browse by Communities, Industries, or Employers.

Career Search Engines

These are services that search sources of employment listings, either job banks like Monster.com or employer websites, and then compile the results of their searching into a single metaindex. Users search these sites by keyword and location, and even browse by location and industry or job family, but in all cases selecting a specific listing to review takes the user back to the original source for review and application. These services can save users a tremendous amount of time that might be spent searching several job sites to find possibilities, but users might also encounter a number of false hits and/or missing listings as the original sites update and delete listings. Despite this, these search engines permit individuals to do these searches in a more efficient manner. Each allows the user to create a free user profile to save searches and create alerts. All of these sites cover countries beyond the United States.

CareerJet	*Indeed*	*SimplyHired*
careerjet.com	indeed.com	simplyhired.com

Resources for Diverse Audiences

There are numerous good career websites focused on specific audiences based on their gender, ethnicity, or faith, offering advice, resources, and even jobs targeted to these people. This list is a very minimal representation of the available resources for consideration.

blackcollegian.com. The Black Collegian Online is a career and job site for African-American college students and is a companion to the print publication distributed to campuses all over the United States. Like the free magazine, this free website offers African-American and other students of color information on careers, job opportunities, graduate and professional schools, internships, study abroad programs, and much more. This site and the magazine are published by IMDiversity, Inc., who also operates the IMDiversity.com website, below.

feminist.org/911/jobs/joblisting.asp. Founded in 1987, the Feminist Majority Foundation (FMF) is dedicated to women's equality, reproductive health, and nonviolence. The jobs and internships posted here include opportunities with academic institutions, nonprofit organizations, and other associations that also support the FMF mission. In addition, there are some opportunities in nontraditional career fields such as law enforcement and construction. This free site is open to all visitors.

imdiversity.com. IMDiversity is a one-stop career and self-development site devoted to serving the cultural and career-related needs of all minorities. This is an excellent resource for all minority and diversity candidates. The many "villages" include resources and information specific for each group, and those without a separate village can find information in the global village. Their job board offers the ability to simultaneously search among featured job opportunities with diversity-committed employers and conduct a second search on a greatly expanded selection of "Network Jobs." Users who create a free account can store a resume here along with preferred searches and more. IMDiversity, Inc. also publishes The Black Collegian.

isna.net/Services/pages/Career-at-ISNA.aspx. This free listing includes jobs with the Islamic Society of North America (ISNA) as well as jobs posted by other organizations, not all of which are connected with the Muslim faith. Applicants are free to review the announcements and apply directly to the hiring organization according to the instructions given.

latpro.com. Started in 1997, LatPro is dedicated to Hispanic and bilingual professionals (Spanish/English and Portuguese/English). LatPro.com offers a searchable resume database and job postings including e-mail alerts. The site is available in English, Spanish, and Portuguese.

lgbtcareerlink.com. Operated by Out and Equal Workplace Advocates in San Francisco, LGBT CareerLink offers visitors and users the opportunity to view job opportunities from a broad variety of diversity-friendly employers, review career resources, and learn about upcoming events for the LGBT community. Most areas of the site are available to all, but individuals are encouraged to register for free and, if desired, create a full profile, upload a resume, and connect with other registered users and employers. This is a very active career and job site filled with good opportunities.

ou.org/jobs. The OU Job Board, The Orthodox Union is a free source of job listings for the U.S., Canada, and Israel, many of which are in Jewish faith-based organizations. Job seekers are also welcome to create a free account and upload a resume, but it is not necessary. This site is operated by The Union of Orthodox Jewish Congregations of America, more popularly known as the Orthodox Union (OU), one of the oldest Orthodox Jewish organizations in the United States. The main website connects with additional social services offered by this organization.

nativejobs.com. Founded in 1996, *The Tribal Employment Newsletter* is a nationwide job bank for Native Americans seeking professional and technical opportunities. There are numerous job listings at any time, and the listings are constantly updated. There is no registration for the site; everything is free and easily accessible.

Resources and Services for Ex-Offenders

Many offenders have great difficulty finding permanent employment after release due to a lack of job-seeking experience, a work history, and occupational skills. These individuals also face the reality that many employers refuse to hire individuals with criminal records. There are organizations and services dedicated to this group, but they can be difficult to find once an individual is released from incarceration. These resources will help users find those organizations and also provide some tools to aid possible clients.

fcnetwork.org. Founded in 1983, The Family and Corrections Network is the first national organization in the United States focused on families of the incarcerated. The website includes links to numerous local groups offering services and support to the incarcerated and their families during and after their separation.

hirenetwork.org. Established by the Legal Action Center, the National HIRE Network is a national clearinghouse for information as well as an advocate for policy change. The goal of this organization is to increase the number and quality of job opportunities available to people with criminal records by changing public policies, employment practices, and public opinion. The Network also provides training and technical assistance to agencies working to improve the employment prospects for people with criminal records. Practitioners can use the Resources list to find state agencies and local organizations to assist clients and practitioners.

nicic.gov. The National Institute of Corrections is an agency of the U. S. Department of Justice and the Federal Bureau of Prisons that provides training, technical assistance, information services, and policy/program development assistance to federal, state, and local corrections agencies. NIC also provides leadership to influence correctional policies, practices, and operations nationwide in areas of emerging interest and concern to correctional executives and practitioners as well as public policymakers. For counselors and other career practitioners working with this group, there are numerous free documents and products available to assist clients as well as practitioners.

nicic.gov/Library/023066. This bulletin, *Career Resource Centers: An Emerging Strategy for Improving Offender Employment Outcomes, National Institute of Corrections,* provides a step-by-step guide for setting up a Career Resource Center in a correctional facility, a parole or probation office, or a community-based organization. It includes a companion multimedia DVD that contains many of the resources needed to operate an effective center, including assessment software and documents related to career exploration, offender re-entry, collaboration building and more.

nicic.gov/Library/022996. This CD-ROM, *Simulated Online/Kiosk Job Application, National Institute of Corrections,* can be used to practice completing employment applications on a computer that does not have access to the Internet. This simulation training program provides basic information about computerized employment applications on kiosks, tips for completing online job applications, a printable worksheet that can be used to prepare offenders for using these systems, and a full-length interactive application with context sensitive help.

rileyguide.com/kiosk.html. Many ex-offenders are not familiar with the online applications and electronic application kiosks in use today, limiting their ability to apply for jobs. This page of the Riley Guide links to several free resources and services clients and practitioners can use to develop a familiarity with application kiosks and online job applications and even develop a printed application an individual can carry along as a guide when submitting applications through in-house application kiosks. This is part of The Riley Guide's collection of articles on How to Job Search (rileyguide.com/execute.html).

Resources and Services for Youth, Teens, and Young Adults

Learning about careers can begin at a very early age, and there are many good free resources designed for different age groups. Some of the best career exploration resources online have been developed by various state education and employment agencies and offer targeted information for their locations. In addition to this short list, some of the resources listed under Occupational Information, above, also offer materials for these groups.

bls.gov/k12. Those who work with students in grades 4–8 will appreciate BLS Kids and the introductory career information offered in this simplified version of the *Occupational Outlook Handbook* (OOH). According to the Bureau of Labor Statistics (BLS), "wording and labor market concepts have been simplified and some statistical detail has been eliminated. In addition, the occupations on the site are categorized according to interests and hobbies common among students." The Teacher's Guide offers more information on this site, how it differs from the full OOH, and additional resources available from BLS.

cacareerzone.org. California CareerZone is a terrific career exploration and planning system designed especially for students in California, but it can be used by others to begin discusses and exploration. The option of selecting text, graphic, or Flash versions makes it easily accessible by users on any kind of online connection. Users are encouraged to work through the Interest Profiler, Work Importance Profiler, and Assess Yourself assessment based on the Holland Codes for self-exploration. Comprehensive information on 900 occupations includes state specific wages, worker attributes, job characteristics, and much more. The Reality Check is a great introduction to the concept of how much money is needed for life after high school and will really open some eyes. Users do not need to register, but it is free and will allow them to save their data to a profile.

dcjobsource.com/fedinterns.html. From this page users can link to internship opportunities available in each agency or department of the Federal Government. The page also includes links to all members of the U.S. House of Representatives and the U.S. Senate who offer internships in their DC or home offices.

march2success.com. A public service of the United States Army, March 2 Success is a web-based program designed to assist high school students in the ninth grade and above improve their performance on tests of math, science, and English, ACT and SAT preparation, state standardized tests, and their overall test-taking skills. There is no set number of tests each user can access, and tests can be retaken until the user is comfortable with the results. The program is free and completely confidential. Users will not be contacted by Army recruiters unless that contact is specifically requested. Content for the various tools was provided by Peterson's, Educational Options, and the College Options Foundation.

ncda.org. The National Career Development Association and Junior Achievement Inc. have jointly developed resources to teach students about the world of work and encourage them to engage in the career planning process. These resources are available to practitioners at no charge and are organized by education level and setting. The documents are in PDF format and are freely accessible to all.

- Urban Elementary (ncda.org/pdf/ElementaryUrbanv2.pdf)
- Elementary (ncda.org/pdf/Elementaryv2.pdf)

- Middle School (ncda.org/pdf/MiddleGradesv2.pdf)
- High School (ncda.org/pdf/HighSchoolv2.pdf)

onedayonejob.com. One Day, One Job is a blog about entry-level jobs. Every day, author Willy Franzen and his collaborators look at one employer and the jobs offered for recent college graduates, examining both online and offline media for information on jobs that may be overlooked because the employers are not part of the top companies that hire at the entry level. Visitors to this free site will also find job search advice and a similar examination of internships (One Day, One Internship—onedayoneinternship.com).

urbanemploy.com. Urban Employ Network is a source for internships and jobs in major cities across the United States. Visitors can view basic data on the actual job postings without registering, but to see full data and apply for the opportunities users must register and upload a resume (free). This will only be necessary on one site as it will copy to the others in the network, but users must search each city's site separately. This site partners with IdeaList.org to stream relevant listings, but it also offers many direct postings from employers. The site offers some premium resources for a fee, but it is not really necessary to use these.

youth.gc.ca; jeunesse.gc.ca. Youth Canada/Jeunesse Canada was created to help prepare young people for the workplace and the job hunt. Youth Canada/Jeunesse Canada is a partnership among several agencies of the Canadian government and the private sector. Visitors to this website will find self-assessment tools and career resources, along with job opportunities and resources for starting a business. This site is available in both English and French. Users from other countries will need to refer back to relevant local resources for specific information on occupations and laws, but this is an excellent introduction to life after school and all of its possibilities.

Resources for the Older Client

Older clients might not be looking for new employment as much as a new purpose in life. While this list offers some job resources and job search advice, it also includes resources for those who are more interested in finding a new opportunity to engage in life and career.

encore.org. Encore Careers encourages older persons to pursue second careers to provide personal fulfillment doing paid work and producing a windfall of human talent to solve society's problems. There are no jobs listed but there are examples, suggestions, fellowships, and an extensive network of like-minded individuals who have been there and done that and are now interested in making a change in a way that serves society and others. This site is operated by Civic Ventures, a group working to engage the baby boomer generation as a vital workforce for change.

ilostmyjob.com. This site is designed to support persons in transition, either voluntarily or involuntarily. The site is filled with good articles on surviving the transition and executing a job search, and also provides links to resources such as state job banks and unemployment claims offices. Registered members get early notifications of new videos and articles posted on the site as well as email newsletters. Robert Shindell is general manager and the iLostmyJob.com Career Doctor.

job-hunt.org/job-search-networking/job-search-networking.shtml. This collection of listings for all 50 states plus the District of Columbia will help users find and connect with local networking and support groups while searching for new or better opportunities. From this page, users can also access lists of company/corporate, military, and government "alumni" groups as well as a list of more than 1,500 professional associations and societies by industry.

whatsnext.com. This organization provides information, inspiration and resources for men and women interested in changing careers, finding more fulfilling work, or improving their work-life balance. While all are welcome, there is an emphasis on those who are in midcareer or approaching retirement. This site includes advice on second careers (Career 2.0), financial planning, and a searchable directory of advisors who can assist with your career change or life plans. Under "Tools" is a collection of free and fee-based assessment tools and financial planning calculators along with links to some very good jobs for experienced professionals. Not everything is free, but there is a lot of good advice and resources available here.

aarp.org/work/. This is a collection of articles and resources covering various topics in work and employment for older people. Issues discussed include discrimination, career changes, retirement, and starting your own business. While looking at these resources, take some time to look at AARP's National Employer Team, a list of member organizations who recognize the value of the more experienced worker and actively recruit and hire older workers.

Resources for the People with Disabilities

These free resources offer specific programs and services designed to match individuals with disabilities with opportunities and employers who are interested in their abilities.

aapd.com. According to their website, the American Association of People with Disabilities (AAPD) is the largest national nonprofit cross-disability member organization in the United States, dedicated to ensuring economic self-sufficiency and political empowerment for the more than 50 million Americans with disabilities. The site includes two listings of internship programs for disabled youth:

1. Under "Programs," users will find the AAPD Internships with congressional and federal summer programs in Washington, DC.
2. Under "Disability Resources," users will find a listing of Other Internships, programs from other organizations which are open to and encourage applications from persons with disabilities. Select a program to be connected to its information.

afb.org/careerconnect. CareerConnect is a free resource of the American Foundation for the Blind where the blind or visually impaired can learn about the range and diversity of the jobs performed throughout the United States and Canada by other who are blind or visually impaired. CareerConnect takes the user through the process of examining what he or she has to offer an employer. Users explore careers, review tips on finding work, getting hired, and making that job work, and examine information on technology to assist in the job. Users can even build a resume online in MyCareerConnect and search for a volunteer mentor to offer some guidance while proceeding through the exploration and search. Finally, users can link to resources for employment listings. All visitors can read the articles and search the databases, but to contact a mentor or set up My CareerConnect, an individual must fill out the free registration form.

ehrweb.aaas.org/entrypoint. Entry Point is a program of the American Association for the Advancement of Science (AAAS) that offers students with disabilities outstanding internship opportunities in science, engineering, mathematics, computer science, and some fields of business. Application and program information is available on the site.

gettinghired.com. This is a free website designed to create employment opportunities for people with disabilities. Several very good employers are associated with this resource and the database is well populated with opportunities. Users must register in order to view any piece of the real site, including the job listings, and in some cases the user must have "an active jobseeker profile" (a resume) in the system in order to use resources such as the career assessment. However, for those who have disabilities this looks like a terrific site and offers great jobs.

hireds.com. Hire Disability Solutions is an organization that works to empower individuals with disabilities to reach their goals by providing them with the tools to succeed. The website presents information and resources for individuals to connect with employers and build their skills, allowing them to discover the feeling of accomplishment. Partnering with several related nonprofit organizations, numerous corporations, and Monster.com, this full-service staffing and consulting firm works to assist individuals to find meaningful employment while also aiding employers in finding the very best staffing for their companies. Individuals can easily search the database of employment opportunities and view contact information for the posting organization, but a user will need to create a Monster.com account in order to apply for these positions. Users can also post a resume on the HireDS.com site by completing their quick registration (name, e-mail address, and a password).

Resources to Aid Separating Military Personnel and Veterans

After years of service, men and women in the armed forces who wish to pursue new careers in the private sector need assistance in adapting to a different culture and in matching their extensive skills and experiences to civilian jobs. There are numerous government-sponsored and civilian resources and services available to them for free and numerous employers searching for these experienced individuals.

civilianjobs.com. Owned by Bradley-Morris Inc., CivilianJobs.com was created to offer an online recruiting solution for candidates that are currently transitioning out of the military as well as military veterans with varying amounts of business experience. There are numerous good job listings posted here, and the organization sponsors a number of live career fairs across the country on a regular basis. Under Career Advice, The Career Planning Guide is a good map to a successful transition.

militarytocivilian.com. This is an extensive blog devoted to helping transitioning military and prior-military persons find careers in the civilian world. Articles posted here include resume tips, how to translate your military experience into terms a civilian hiring authority can understand, hot career areas for military-experienced job seekers, career coaching, and more. This blog is authored by Jessica Richardson, a graduate of the U.S. Naval Academy, and is supported by Bradley-Morris Inc.

rileyguide.com/vets.html. This page of The Riley Guide, Resources for Veterans and Military Personnel and Their Families, is dedicated to sites, services, and resources that support current and former military personnel and their families. Along with job search advice and resources it also lists information for employers who want to attract these qualified candidates, information on pay rates and employment verification, and employment and financial rights for reservists called to active duty.

job-hunt.org/article_veterans_jobsearch.shtml. This section of Job-Hunt.org, The Veteran's Job Search, begins with an extensive article on how to make the transition from the military to the civilian workforce and then points the reader towards several additional articles and resources for guidance. It is authored by Job-Hunt.org editor and publisher Susan Joyce, a veteran of the U.S. Marine Corps.

Resources for Specific Industries and Occupations

A list of resources dedicated to providing information about a specific industry or occupational field is provided in this section. The primary focus of this list is career information, but most of the sites also provide job listings, education information, lists of potential employers, salary guides, and resume databases. While several sites may require the user to create an account in order to use the full potential of the resources, particularly posting of resumes, these resources and activities were free at the time of this review. All users should be reminded to review the privacy policies of the sites services with which they are registering and be cautious about sharing any personal information not required by law (such as a Social Security Number and date of birth).

Agriculture and Forestry

American Society of Agronomy
  agronomy.org
The National FFA Organization (Future Farmers of America)
  ffa.org
Tree Care Industry Association
  treecareindustry.org

Art, Culture, and Design

Dance
  Dance Magazine
    dancemagazine.com
Fashion
  Careers from Women's Wear Daily
    wwd.com/wwdcareers/
Graphics / Creative Media
  The Professional Association for Design
    aiga.org
  The Association for Computing Machinery's Special Interest Group on Graphics and Interactive Techniques
    siggraph.org
  Communication Arts Network
    commarts.com
History
  American Historical Association
    historians.org
Museum and Art Exhibit Management
  American Association of Museums
    aam-us.org
Music/Music Education
  Careers in Music, Berklee College of Music
    berklee.edu/careers
  The Savvy Musician
    savvymusician.com
  The National Association for Music Education
    menc.org
Theater Production
  BackstageJobs.com

Business, Administration, and Financial

Accounting and Finance
  American Institute for Certified Public Accountants
    aicpa.org
  Association for Finance Professionals
    afponline.org
Actuaries
  Actuary.com
  American Academy of Actuaries
    actuary.org
Appraisals
  American Society of Appraisers
    appraisers.org
  Appraisal Institute
    appraisalinstitute.org
Human Resources/Training and Development
  American Society for Training and Development
    astd.org
  Society for Human Resource Management
    shrm.org
Marketing
  Marketing Today
    marketingtoday.com
  MarketingPower, from the American Marketing Association
    marketingpower.com
Public Relations
  Public Relations Society of America
    prsa.org

Commercial Services

Convention and Meeting Management
  Professional Convention Management Association
    pcma.org

Commercial Services Continued

Packaging
  Women in Packaging
    womeninpackaging.org
Purchasing and Supply Management
  American Purchasing Society
    american-purchasing.com
  Institute for Supply Management
    ism.ws
Real Estate & Property Management
  The Institute of Real Estate Management
    irem.org
  National Association of Industrial and Office
  Properties
    naiop.org

Building, Construction, and Mining

Building/Construction
  American Public Works Association
    apwa.net
  Associated Builders and Contractors
    abc.org
  Blue Collar and Proud of It! Success Outside
  the Cubicle
    bluecollarandproudofit.com
  Helmets to Hardhats
    helmetstohardhats.org
  Mike Rowe WORKS
    mikeroweworks.com
  Home Builders Institute
    hbi.org
    buildingcareers.org
Chimney Sweep
  National Chimney Sweep Guild
    ncsg.org
Electricians
  National Electrical Contractors Association
    necanet.org
Mining
  InfoMine
    Infomine.com
  The Society for Mining, Metallurgy, and
  Exploration
    smenet.org

Education, Instruction, and Information Management

Education/Administration
  American College Personnel Association
    myacpa.org

Education, Instruction, and Information Continued

  American Society for Engineering Education
    asee.org
  Chronicle of Higher Education
    chronicle.com
  PhDs.org
    www.phds.org
  The Council for Exceptional Children
    specialedcareers.org
  Troops to Teachers
    www.dantes.doded.mil/dantes_
    web/troopstoteachers/index.asp
  USA K-12 Employment Opportunities, the
  University of Kentucky's College of Education
    education.uky.edu/AcadServ/
    content/employment
Information Management and Library Science
  American Library Association
    ala.org
  ALA Allied Professional Association
    ala-apa.org
  ARMA International (records and information
  management)
    arma.org
  LISjobs.com
    lisjobs.com

Engineering, Architecture, and Mathematics

General Resources
  Institution of Engineering and Technology
    theiet.org
  National Society of Professional Engineers
    nspe.org
  Sloan Career Cornerstone Center
    careercornerstone.org
Aeronautics/Astronautics
  See also Aviation and Aerospace under
  Transportation
  American Institute of Aeronautics and
  Astronautics
    aiaa.org
  European Space Agency
    esa.int
  NASA
    nasa.gov
Architecture and Planning
  American Institute of Architects
    aia.org

*Engineering, Architecture and
Mathematics Continued*

American Planning Association
planning.org
American Society of Landscape Architects
asla.org
ARCHcareers.org
The Royal Institute of British Architects
architecture.com
Automotive Engineering
The Society of Automotive Engineers
sae.org
National Automotive Technicians Education
Foundation
natef.org
Bioengineering/Biotechnology
Biomedical Engineering Society
bmes.org
Nanowerk
nanowerk.com
Society for Biological Engineering
aiche.org/SBE/
Chemical Engineering
The American Institute of Chemical Engineers
aiche.org
Civil Engineering
American Society of Civil Engineers
asce.org
Computing and Technology
Association for Computing Machinery
acm.org
ComputerWorld
computerworld.com
Webgrrls International
webgrrls.com
Women in Technology International
witi.com
Electrical Engineering
Institute of Electrical and Electronics Engineers
ieee.org
Explosives Engineering/Pyrotechnics
International Society of Explosives Engineers
isee.org
Pyrotechnics Guild International
pgi.org
The World of Explosives
explosives.org
Facility Engineering/Plant Maintenance
FacilitiesNet
facilitiesnet.com

*Engineering, Architecture and
Mathematics Continued*

Association for Facilities Engineering
afe.org
Fire Protection Engineering
Society of Fire Protection Engineers
sfpe.org
National Fire Protection Association
nfpa.org
Industrial Design
Core77 Industrial Design Magazine and
Resource
core77.com
The Industrial Designers Society of America
idsa.org
Instrumentation/Control/Automation
International Society of Automation
isa.org
Materials
American Ceramic Society
ceramics.org
ASM International, The Materials Information
Society
asminternational.org
Mathematics
American Mathematical Society
ams.org
Society for Industrial and Applied Mathematics
siam.org
Mechanical Engineering
The American Society of Mechanical Engineers
www.asme.org
Naval Engineering
American Society of Naval Engineers
navalengineers.org
Occupational/Environmental Health and Safety
American Industrial Hygiene Association
aiha.org
Optics/Photonics
The Optical Society
osa.org
The Society of Photo-Optical Instrumentation
Engineers
spie.org
Surveying and Mapping
American Congress on Surveying and Mapping
acsm.net
National Council of Examiners for Engineering
and Surveying
ncees.org

Government, Public Service, and Nonprofit Opportunities

Development/Fund Raising
  Chronicle of Philanthropy
    Philanthropy.com
Government
  Careers in Government
    careersingovernment.com
  Careers in National Defense, U.S. Department
  of Defense
    godefense.com
  USAJobs, U.S. Office of Personnel Management
    usajobs.gov
  Women In Defense, a National Security
  Organization
    wid.ndia.org
Nonprofit
  Jobs for Change from Change.org
    jobs.change.org
  OpportunityKnocks.org
Public Policy/Public Affairs
  Foreign Policy Association
    fpa.org
  PublicServiceCareers.org
    publicservicecareers.org
  Careers with the U.S. Department of State
    careers.state.gov
  Women in Government Relations
    wgr.org

Healthcare and Medicine

General Resources
  The Association of American Medical Colleges
    aspiringdocs.org
  American Dental Education Association
    explorehealthcareers.org
  NEJM Career Center, New England Journal of
  Medicine
    nejmjobs.org
Chiropractics
  International Chiropractors Association
    chiropractic.org
Dental Care
  American Dental Association
    ada.org
Diet and Nutrition
  American Dietetic Association
    eatright.org
  American Society for Nutrition
    nutrition.org

Healthcare and Medicine Continued

Fitness/Sports Medicine
  American College of Sports Medicine
    acsm.org
  American Council on Exercise
    acefitness.org
  National Strength and Conditioning
  Association
    nsca-lift.org
Gerontology/Geriatrics
  The Gerontological Society of America
    geron.org
Nursing
  American College of Nurse-Midwives
    midwife.org
  American Nurses Association
    nursingworld.org
Orthotics and Prosthetics
  American Academy of Orthotists & Prosthetists
    oandp.org
Pharmacy
  American Pharmacists Association
    pharmacist.com
Public Health
  American Public Health Association
    apha.org
  Association of Schools of Public Health
    asph.org
Rehabilitative Therapies
  American Massage Therapy Association
    amtamassage.org
  American Occupational Therapy Association
    aota.org

Hospitality and Recreation

Culinary
  American Culinary Federation
    acfchefs.org
  American Personal & Private Chef Association
    personalchef.com
Hospitality
  Hcareers
    hcareers.com
  DiversityInHospitality.com
  WomenInHospitality.com
Outdoor Activities
  CoolWorks
    coolworks.com
Sports
  The Sporting Goods Manufacturers Association
    sgma.com

Hospitality and Recreation Continued

Women's Sports Foundation
womenssportsfoundation.org
Travel Agents
American Society of Travel Agents
asta.org

Law Enforcement and Protective Services

Fire Investigators
InterFIRE
interfire.org
International Association of Arson
Investigators
firearson.com
Law Enforcement
911hotjobs.com
The International Association of
Chiefs of Police
discoverpolicing.org
Security and Asset Management
American Society for Industrial Security
asisonline.org

Lawyers and Other Legal Services

Arbitration
American Arbitration Association
adr.org
Court Reporters/Captioners
National Court Reporters Association
ncraonline.org
Lawyers
American Bar Association
abanet.org
Association of Corporate Counsel
acc.com
Paralegals
The National Federation of Paralegal
Associations
paralegals.org

Manufacturing, Mechanical Repair, and Precision Craft

Fishing/Seafood Processing
Seafood and Fishing Jobs in Alaska: What Crew
Members On Board Fishing Vessels in Alaska
Need to Know, Alaska Division of Employment
Security
labor.state.ak.us/esd_alaska_jobs/
seafood.htm

Manufacturing, Mechanical Repair and Precision Craft Continued

Seafood Processing Jobs in Alaska, Alaska
Division of Employment Security
labor.state.ak.us/esd_alaska_jobs/process.htm
Musical Instrument Repair
National Association of Professional Band
Instrument Repair Technicians
napbirt.org
Piano Technicians Guild
ptg.org
Welding/Metalforming
Precision Metalforming Association
pma.org
Wood Products
The Association of Woodworking &
Furnishing Suppliers
woodindustryed.org

Natural Sciences

General Resources
NewScientist
newscientist.com
Science Careers
sciencecareers.sciencemag.org
Animal Sciences
American Veterinary Medical Association
avma.org
Association of American Veterinary Medical
Colleges
aavmc.org
American Society of Limnology and
Oceanography
aslo.org
Association of Zoos and Aquariums
aza.org
Astronomy
American Astronomical Society
aas.org
Biology
American Institute of Biological Sciences
aibs.org
American Society for Investigative Pathology
asip.org
Chemistry
American Chemical Society
acs.org

Natural Sciences Continued

Earth, Conservation, and Environmental Sciences
  Earth Science World
    earthscienceworld.org
  EnvironmentalCareer.com
  Green Industry Job Search Guide
    Job-Hunt.org
    job-hunt.org/green-jobs-job-search/
    green-jobs.shtml
  International Institute for Sustainable
  Development
    iisd.org
Entomology
  Entomological Society of America
    entsoc.org
Forensics
  American Academy of Forensic Sciences
    aafs.org
Geography
  Association of American Geographers
    aag.org
Geology
  American Association of Petroleum Geologists
    aapg.org
  American Institute of Professional Geologists
    aipg.org
  Society of Exploration Geophysicists
    seg.org
Meteorology
  American Meteorological Society
    ametsoc.org
Natural Resources
  Cyber-Sierra's Natural Resources Job Search
    cyber-sierra.com/nrjobs/
Ocean Sciences
  The Centers for Ocean Sciences Education
  Excellence
    oceancareers.com
Ornithology
  American Ornithologists' Union
    aou.org
Physics
  American Association of Physics Teachers
    aapt.org
  American Physical Society
    aps.org
Water Quality
  American Water Works Association
    awwa.org
  Work for Water
    workforwater.org

Personal Services

Caregivers
  Sittercity
    sittercity.com
  Childcare.gov
  How to Offer Child-Care Services
    Entrepreneur.com
    entrepreneur.com/startingabusiness/
    businessideas/startupkits/article41422-1.
    html
Personal Care
  Behind The Chair
    www.behindthechair.com
Pet Care
  National Association of Professional Pet Sitters
    petsitters.org
Professional Organizer
  National Association of Professional Organizers
    napo.net

Social Science Fields

Anthropology
  American Anthropological Association
    aaanet.org
Archaeology
  The Archaeological Institute of America
    archaeological.org
Counseling/Psychology
  American Association for Marriage and Family
  Therapy
    aamft.org
  American Counseling Association
    counseling.org
  American Psychological Association
    apa.org
  American School Counselor Association
    schoolcounselor.org
  National Career Development Association
    ncda.org
Economics
  American Economic Association Job Openings
  for Economists
    aeaweb.org/joe
Languages/Linguistics
  American Translators Association
    atanet.org
  Linguist List
    linguistlist.org
  Registry of Interpreters for the Deaf
    rid.org
Social Work/Social Services
  The National Association of Social Workers
    socialworkers.org

Transportation and Logistics

Aviation/Aerospace
*See also Aeronautics/Astronautics
under Engineering*
AviationWeek.com
Flightglobal.com, from Reed Business
Information
flightglobal.com
Mariners/Seafarers
American Waterways Operators
americanwaterways.com
Maritime Administration, U.S. Department of
Transportation
marad.dot.gov
The Seafarers International Union
seafarers.org
U.S. Merchant Marine Academy
usmma.edu

Utilities and Telecommunications

Energy Providers
American Gas Association
aga.org
American Petroleum Institute
api.org
Interstate Natural Gas Association of America
ingaa.org
Fuel Cell and Hydrogen Energy Association
fchea.org
Nuclear Street
nuclearstreet.com
Telecommunications
US Telecom
ustelecom.org

Writing, Broadcasting, and Media

Broadcasting/Media
Employment in the Media
MediaCollege.com
mediacollege.com/employment/
MediaJobMarket
mediajobmarket.com
National Association of Broadcasters
nab.org
Variety Media Careers
Varietymediacareers.com
Journalism
JournalismJobs.com
CubReporters.org
PoynterOnline, The Poynter Institute
poynter.org

Writing, Broadcasting, and Media Continued

Photography/Photojournalism
National Press Photographers Association
nppa.org
The Professional Photographers of America
ppa.com
Publishing
Publishers Weekly
publishersweekly.com
The Association of American Publishers
bookjobs.com
Writing/Technical Writing
American Society of Journalists and Authors
asja.org
National Writers Union
nwu.org
Society for Technical Communications
stc.org
Writers Guild of America
wga.org

Military Service – United States Armed Forces

Today's Military
Todaysmilitary.com
The National Guard
nationalguard.com
www.ng.mil
U.S. Air Force
airforce.com
www.af.mil
U.S. Army
goarmy.com
www.army.mil
U.S. Coast Guard
gocoastguard.com
www.uscg.mil
U.S. Marine Corps
marines.com
www.marines.mil
U.S. Merchant Marine Academy
usmma.edu
U.S. Navy
navy.com
navy.mil

Researching Employers

Learning about employers is an important part of the job search. Knowing who employs persons in this field creates a list of potential targets for a job campaign. Learning that a particular employer is involved in a new line of work means new employment opportunities. Having all of this data in-hand during an interview means the employer is presented with a highly skilled candidate who can match his or her experience to the employer's immediate needs. Knowledge is power, especially when it comes to the job search. The sites listed below will guide users through the research process and offer useful data for the job seeker involved in the process.

libguides.rutgers.edu/companies. The Rutgers librarians have created a company research guide resource to assist individuals seeking to learn about a company. Listings for the top business research sources (both print and online) are provided, and the site is organized by the logical steps of the research process. The research process cites both online and print resources. Users outside of Rutgers should check with their local public or college library for access.

hoovers.com. Hoover's is a well-known and respected publisher of business almanacs. Users can access a tremendous amount of free information from the website, but paid subscribers will have access to more detailed profiles. Hoovers covers U.S. and non-U.S. companies as well as Initial Public Offerings through IPO Central (hoovers.com/ipo-central/100004160-1.html). Individuals should check with a local public or college library to inquire about free access before purchasing this on their own.

vault.com. Vault is a resource for career management and job search information, including insider intelligence on specific employers, salaries, hiring practices, and company cultures. The website offers both free and paid subscription content to users who want to research employers, professions, and industries. There is a public job bank; users will need to create a free basic account to apply for positions listed here. Vault still publishes numerous print guides to various careers, employers, and industries.

wetfeet.com. Wetfeet offers "insider guides to employers" which consist of interviews with employees of the organization or the employers themselves. The guides offer good insights into the company's culture, interview process, and career development possibilities. Wetfeet allows all users to view extensive employer, career, and industry profiles, only sending users to the shop for their detailed print guides at the very end. Most users will gain much from the public information.

Summary

This chapter discusses the variety of online resources and services available to career practitioners and their clients. Career practitioners are encouraged to create online career resource centers (OCRC) for their clients as a way to enhance services, encourage exploration, and guide users to the resources best suited for their needs. When developing an OCRC, it is important that the practitioner plan the project, identifying the target audience, the types of resources to be included, the visual design of the site, how the information will be presented, and how the site will be maintained and continually developed. It is important to select not only the best but the most useful resources for the audience, ensuring that these meet established professional standards while also being worthy of the practitioner's personal recommendation. This chapter includes a sample list of resources that services practitioners may consider for inclusion in their OCRC as well as additional resource to assist in finding much more.

References

Dikel, M. F. (2010). *How to get listed.* Retrieved from http://www.rileyguide.com/listed.html

Epstein, S. A., & Lenz, J. G. (2008). *Developing and managing career resources.* Broken Arrow, OK: National Career Development Association.

Google Webmaster Central. (2010). *Link schemes.* Retrieved from http://www.google.com/support/webmasters/bin/answer.py?answer=66356

International Federation of Library Associations and Institutions Section on Acquisition and Collection Development. (2001). *Guidelines for a collection development policy using the conspectus model.* Retrieved from http://www.ifla.org/files/acquisition-collection-development/publications/gcdp-en.pdf

The Internet Scout Project. (2010). Selection Criteria. *The scout report.* Retrieved from http://scout.wisc.edu/Reports/selection.php

McKenzie, J. (1997) Why in the World Wide Web? *From now on, 6*(6). Retrieved from http://fno.org/mar97/why.html

National Career Development Association. (January 2006) NCDA *Guidelines for the Use of the Internet for Provision of Career Information and Planning Services.* Retrieved from http://associationdatabase.com/aws/NCDA/pt/sp/guidelines_internet

Sampson, J. P., Jr. (2008). *Designing and implementing career programs: A handbook for effective practice.* Broken Arrow, OK: National Career Development Association.

Sampson, J. P. Jr., Carr, D., Panke, J., Arkin, S., Minvielle, M., & Vernick, S. H. (2003) Enhancing counseling services with Internet websites. *Journal of Technology in Counseling, 3*(1), 1-29. Retrieved from http://jtc.colstate.edu/vol3_1/Sampson/Sampson.htm

Whitfield, E. A, Feller, R., & Wood, C. (Eds.). (2009). *A counselor's guide to career assessment instruments* (5th ed.). Broken Arrow, OK: National Career Development Association.

Chapter 6
POTENTIAL PROBLEMS AND
ETHICAL CONCERNS

The Internet dramatically increases the access individuals have to resources and services for career decision making. The problem, however, is that the career resources and services provided on the Internet vary in quality and appropriateness for different users. A number of ethical issues have the potential to limit the benefits of using the Internet to support career choice. This chapter includes a discussion of the quality of resources and services offered on the Internet, individual readiness for Internet use, the availability of user support when needed, the credentials of resource and service providers, the lack of counselor awareness of local conditions and events, confidentiality and user privacy on the Internet, the equality of access to Internet-based career resources and services, and issues related to distance counseling and social networking sites in career counseling.

Quality of Resources and Services Offered on the Internet

Assume that a person wants to buy a new pair of shoes. At the local shopping mall, numerous stores sell shoes. In examining shoes in each store, it becomes obvious that the quality of shoes available ranges from marginal (or maybe even defective) to excellent. While the cost of each pair of shoes seems to be related to its quality, some shoes seem to be expensive in relation to their quality, while other shoes appear to be an exceptional value. Some of the sales persons appear very knowledgeable, while others appear to know little about the shoes they sell. The Internet functions in a similar manner. The quality of the resources and services available varies from marginal (or even invalid or incompetent) to excellent. Some resources and services offer good value for their cost, while others do not. The competencies of practitioners providing Internet-based supportive services vary from incompetent to exemplary. The problem is that it may be easier to spot a poorly manufactured shoe than to detect poor quality resources and services delivered on the Internet, although the benchmarks provided in Chapter 2 will be helpful. Some assessments delivered on the Internet were originally designed to be used within the context of counseling or instruction where a practitioner is available to help interpret the results. Instruments are validated for a specific use or uses. If a valid instrument is used inappropriately in a different context, the results obtained may be invalid. Other assessments delivered on the Internet have never been validated to make certain that they measure what they say they measure. Individuals may make inappropriate decisions on the basis of results that are questionable.

Information resources can be invalid on the basis of poor research or poor delivery. The research used to create the information may have been flawed and inaccurate or biased. Sometimes individuals are more interested in presenting a predetermined point of view, and they seek information that supports their beliefs. This is a serious problem when the information reinforces gender, race, ethnicity, age, religion, sexual orientation, disability status, obesity, poverty, and immigration status stereotypes, or limits the opportunities of individuals on the basis of their characteristics. Even information that was based on valid research can be rendered invalid by poor delivery. Original source data are often summarized for clarity, and mistakes made in the summarization process can result in incorrect data. Attractive graphics on a website can give an impression of quality that does not really exist.

Individuals' Readiness for Use of Internet-Based Self-Help Resources

Individuals vary in their readiness for career decision making. An individual with high readiness for decision making is likely to make effective use of career resources and services. As a result, a high readiness individual is more likely to benefit from self-help resources such as those available on the Internet that require minimal or no assistance from a practitioner. An individual with low readiness for decision making, however, is not likely to make good use of Internet-based self-help resources and services. Figure 6.1 outlines this concept. (See http://www.career.fsu.edu/techcenter/designing_career_services/basic_concepts/index.html for additional details).

Figure 6.1 Components of Career Readiness

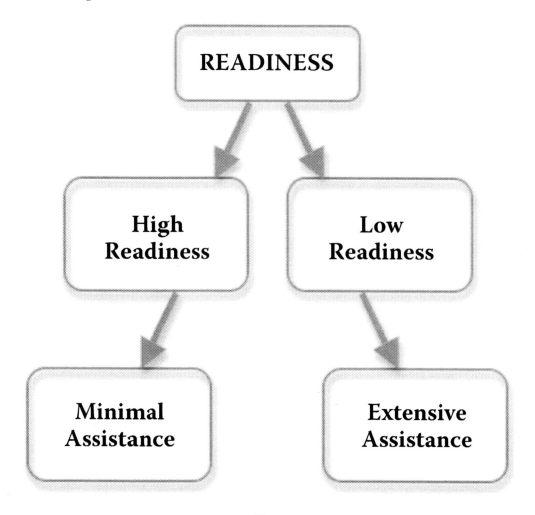

Individuals with low decision-making readiness may be more likely to have a high level of anxiety about making decisions, lack of clarity and instability in their perceptions of self, and negative expectations of their capability to make an appropriate career choice. High levels of anxiety make it more difficult to think clearly about self-knowledge and occupational or employment options. Individuals who have self-perceptions that lack clarity tend to have more difficulty in responding to assessment items and in evaluating the potential appropriateness of an occupation based on a review of occupational information. The same problems tend to hold true for individuals who have self-perceptions that change from day to day. Individuals who do not perceive themselves as capable decision makers are less likely to access and use the career resources and services that are available. As a result, individuals with low readiness for decision making are more likely to make inappropriate use of Internet-based self-help resources or are more likely to discontinue using resources and services because of their frustration over their lack of progress in making a career decision. Specific problems include the following:

- being aware that they have a problem, but being unaware of their needs;
- having unrealistic expectations of the capability of the Internet to solve their career problems;
- being overwhelmed with the potential information available on the Internet;
- having difficulty in selecting information that meets their needs;
- being uncertain about how to make effective use of the information they obtain;
- being uncertain of the options for receiving assistance or obtaining other information resources that may be helpful; and
- having difficulty in understanding information because of the high reading level of text delivered on many sites.

These problems suggest again that the use of Internet-based self-help resources is not appropriate for everyone.

A career practitioner choosing to augment in-session career development services with outside activities such as having the client use the Internet for self-assessment or researching occupations must first assess the client's level of readiness. Chapter 2 describes different levels of client readiness, and the impact of readiness levels on using the Internet for career-related activities. Encouraging a client to use online assessments or tools when the counselor perceives a lack of client readiness to do so may be seen as inappropriate practice as the counselor may be violating the ethical code of doing no harm as described in NCDA ethical code A.4.a (Makela, 2009).

Another issue is related to the process of effective information use, which can be sequenced into the following six steps:

- Recognize that a problem exists and that information is needed.
- Select information to meet identified needs.
- Decide how to use information to meet identified needs.
- Use the information resource (or resources).
- Evaluate whether needs have been met.
- Seek help or other resources as needed until the problem is solved.

Some individuals are more ready than others to use information in making career choices. As a result, some individuals are more likely than others to experience problems in using the Internet to obtain self-help information.

Availability of User Support When Needed

If an individual with limited readiness uses the Internet within the context of a supportive career service, such as a career course, group counseling, or individual counseling (either face-to-face or at a distance), then opportunities exist to help the individual select, sequence, and use Internet-based resources and services. In this case, no ethical problem for use of the Internet exists. If, however, an individual with low readiness does not receive the needed support, then the individual is more likely to make inappropriate use of the Internet.

A basic ethical principle is to do no harm to an individual as a result of the action of the practitioner. Making ineffective use of career resources and services may result in an individual becoming frustrated with a career choice. This frustration may result in the individual making a premature choice as a coping strategy to end a difficult decision-making process. Or, the individual may cope with his or her frustration by procrastinating in the use of career resources and services until external circumstances dictate a choice. Either of these instances may result in harm to the individual. Makela (2009) presents a series of case studies that illustrate these issues in providing career services.

In order to lessen the likelihood of these potential problems, practitioners using the Internet in delivering career resources and services need to take reasonable steps to ensure that the Internet use is appropriate, considering the needs of the individual. A brief screening interview (or in some cases a more comprehensive screening using a readiness screening measure) is one option for helping to determine the potential of a client to profit from getting information in this mode. For example, a practitioner may want to ask the client about comfort and skill with using the Internet as well as access to the Internet. Practitioners may also be at risk of violating this ethical principle if they create and maintain websites that fail to indicate the circumstances where problems may occur in self-help use or those that require the potential assistance of a practitioner.

Credentials of Resource and Service Providers on the Internet

Currently, the credentials of individuals who are delivering career resources and services on the Internet tend to be either vague or not stated. Sometimes the educational degree of the developer is identified, for example, PhD, but the degree field is not indicated. While a doctoral degree in chemistry is very relevant to conducting chemical research, a chemist with only these credentials would not be able to obtain licensure or certification as a counselor and may not have the skills required to deliver effective counseling services. Listing a degree without indicating the field of study is misleading at best and fraudulent at worst. It is important to acknowledge that a small number of resource and service providers have clearly indicated their credentials. While credentialing provides no guarantee of eliminating incompetence or malpractice, it does reduce the probability that unqualified individuals will offer Internet-based resources and services to the public. Some qualifications to look for would include level of degree (e.g., BA/BS, MA/MS, EdD/PhD), program of study (e.g., counseling, career counseling, vocational psychology), and national certifications or licenses (e.g., CDF/GCDF, NBCC, LPC, LMHC) along with the license or certification number.

The skills required for the development of career resources and the delivery of career services share both similarities and differences. Both career resource and service tasks require an understanding of the content and process of career development. Developing career resources for a website may require skills in assessment or labor market analysis. Information about the developer's training and experience in psychometrics in the first case or library science or economics for the second case would be very appropriate. When delivering career services at a distance, practitioners should document credentialing in counseling or a related field. This is especially important given the interconnectedness of career and mental health issues. One trend in professional standards for distance counseling is to require that the service deliverer be appropriately credentialed for practice in at least one jurisdiction, such as licensure to practice in at least one state.

Lack of Practitioner Awareness of Local Conditions and Events

Distance counseling provides important opportunities to provide career services to individuals in geographically remote or underserved locations. A problem can occur, however, when a career practitioner is unaware of how local economic conditions (such as supply and demand for workers in the local labor market) or recent events (such as a plant closing) potentially influence the career choices of a client. Such lack of awareness may limit practitioner credibility or result in inappropriate counseling interventions. Career practitioners need to prepare for counseling in a geographically remote location by becoming familiar with recent conditions and events in that area.

Confidentiality and User Privacy on the Internet

The potential for violation of confidentiality already exists through inappropriate access to client records in print, audio, and video formats. Creating, storing, and retrieving client records on computers with Internet connections compounds confidentiality problems by increasing the potential for inappropriate access. Potential problems include unauthorized individuals gaining access to a career practitioner's computer where client records are stored or obtaining and using file transmissions of email correspondence, client assessments, and case notes. Career practitioners need to remain aware of potential violations to confidentiality and become familiar with, and consistently use, appropriate security techniques such as changing passwords frequently and encrypting data transmissions sent over the Internet.

Privacy may be compromised during videoconference-based distance counseling if constant distractions negatively impact the counseling process (e.g., being heard, observed, or manipulated by another individual during a session). A similar problem may inadvertently occur at public access points if appropriate auditory and physical privacy is not provided for clients. In addition, knowing that online communications are unsecure, every effort should be made to provide security and to inform the client that the conversations are not completely secure, so that they can determine if they would like to continue using distance counseling or distance advising. Saunders (2007) recommends purchasing text encryption software or using an online platform that provides secure communications as a way to increase security. Career practitioners need to monitor client behavior during counseling to determine if privacy has been violated and, if so, take appropriate steps to remedy the problem.

Equality of Access to Internet-Based Career Resources and Services

At present, access to the Internet is strongly influenced by socioeconomic status. More affluent individuals who have access to the Internet at their place of work and residence enjoy greater access to career resources and services. For example, if they see a website advertised on a billboard, television, or suggested by a friend, they can explore that site and others at their leisure; however, someone with limited Internet access may be constrained to using a computer in a public library which places limits on the types of sites that can be viewed and the time allowed online.

There is a justifiable concern that limited Internet access will increase the income disparity between well-educated, affluent groups and less educated, less affluent groups in our society. While technological improvements are making Internet access easier and less expensive, these developments are occurring slowly. In the interim, career practitioners should support public access to the Internet (such as through free access in shopping mall kiosks and workstations in public libraries) and publicize the availability of such access to relevant populations.

Distance Counseling

Distance counseling is not appropriate for every potential client or practitioner. A career practitioner desiring to offer career planning or counseling services via distance counseling must consider several factors prior to making that decision. Distance career counseling might be synchronous, asynchronous, or both. The individual client's best interest should always be the determining factor when deciding about the appropriateness of distance counseling. A practitioner should consider the client's hardware and software compatibility with the programs required by the practitioner to perform distance counseling. For example, some websites only run in Internet Explorer, virtual worlds are often high in graphics and may require an advanced graphics card, some computers require an external microphone and speakers. Also, the client's experience and comfort with using the tools required for distance counseling should play a factor. A practitioner must also ensure that to every degree possible, a client's confidentiality is protected.

A practitioner considering providing distance counseling should give thought to the following issues and questions before offering online services:

- What are my charges for distance counseling? How will I charge? If I am delivering services mainly through email, how do I determine how much to charge? Do I charge by the email, or offer a package deal where they have unlimited access to me for a period of time?

- What is my policy on counseling those outside of my state? From a legal and ethical standpoint, practitioners should collect enough information from the distance client so that if an emergency arises, the practitioner can contact help that is nearby. Practitioners should be aware of state counseling laws for each client's state.

- What services will I provide via distance counseling? What percentage of my clients will be served online? How will I orient clients on the tools I will be using?

- How will I screen clients to determine if they are appropriate for distance counseling?

- What can I do to protect my client's confidentiality?

- How will I collect payment?

- How will I evaluate my services?

While there are certainly other issues to consider, the ones outlined above are of particular importance when making a decision about providing distance counseling. A comprehensive bibliography on distance counseling (Coughlin, Shy, J. D., Sampson, & Lenz, 2010) is available at http://career.fsu.edu/documents/bibliographies/Dist_Counseling_Biblio_Aug_2010.pdf.

Social Networking

The use of social networking sites (SNSs) such as Facebook, MySpace, LinkedIn, and Twitter are a part of many individuals' every day lives. Many universities, corporations, not-for-profits, and individual practitioners have a presence on one or more of these networks. These sites can serve as a venue for services and also marketing, and they can offer many exciting possibilities for clients and service providers. However, ethical concerns can be raised whenever technology and counseling interface. Specifically, issues of confidentiality and dual relationships are primary concerns.

While associations such as the American Counseling Association (2005), the National Career Development Association (2007), the Association of Computer-Based Systems for Career Information (2006) and the National Board for Certified Counselors (nd) do not have ethical standards specific to social networking sites, it can be assumed that, at a minimum, the same standards that are outlined for face-to-face client relationships would also apply to online relationships. There are some online discussions about whether or not it is ethical to "friend" a client, with the majority leaning towards a negative answer, based on the argument that a practitioner would not go out for coffee with a client or attend the client's birthday party, because that would blur the practitioner-client line and set up a dual relationship. Others in these discussions point out that it might not be improper to use SNSs for marketing purposes or for closed counseling groups. A practitioner using SNSs must disclose that others (such as the technology team on the site) are likely to have access to who is a member of a particular site.

Twitter presents a different issue because a client might choose to "follow" a career practitioner the same as nonclients. While the practitioner has no control over this, it is a good idea to check who is following and bring this up for discussion in the session. Also, a practitioner should be very careful not to tweet about sessions or clients, even anonymously. To tweet "just finished an intense session," or "off to a client session, ugh" is unprofessional and harmful to current and potential clients, and ultimately to the profession.

Adding to the difficulty in making decisions about the use of SNSs and confidentiality is defining who is a client. For example, career centers that have SNS groups, fan pages, Twitter followers, and LinkedIn groups likely have students as fans/followers/friends. These individuals can see others' profiles online, as can employers who are fans/followers/friends of the career center. In this case, has confidentiality been broken? Are all students who use a career center classified as clients? Are students who attend a workshop on resume writing entitled to expect confidentiality from other participants? What if the topic is on choosing a major, or working with diverse populations in the workplace? Does this change if the workshops are online in a synchronous (real time with people chatting verbally or in text) chat?

If a career practitioner decides to use SNSs to deliver services, the practitioner should have a clear purpose and rules of engagement outlined for clients. There are possible ways to use a client's activity in a social networking site during a counseling session. For example, if there is adequate trust and the client agrees, the practitioner and the client might view the client's SNS together as a way to explore how the client's profile or other information (e.g., types of pictures posted) might be impacting the way others view him or her. This would be particularly helpful with a client's LinkedIn account. Other possibilities might include a discussion about a client's blog or comments, exploring the feel of the site, friends' activities that might be useful to hide, and so forth. It does not appear that practitioners are using SNSs to provide career counseling services at this time, but that is very likely to change in the near future as technology continues to advance. As the ethics have not been written specifically for using technology in this way, a practitioner would need to work from the existing ethics, and seek feedback from other professionals before engaging in that activity.

Summary

A main purpose of this book was to introduce the possibilities of Internet resources for use with the career counseling process. In previous chapters, the authors sought to establish the point that simply providing a list of websites to a client was unprofessional. In this chapter, the argument is made that giving a list of links without support is also unethical. Career practitioners should also be aware of ethical issues such as resource and service quality, individual readiness for Internet use, the availability of needed user support, appropriate credentialing of resource and service providers, practitioner awareness of conditions and events in remote counseling locations, confidentiality and user privacy, and equality of access to the Internet. This is the first step in ensuring that use of Internet-based career resources and services results in helping rather than harming the public.

References

American Counseling Association. (2005). *ACA code of ethics.* Retrieved from www.counseling.org/ethics

Association of Computer-Based Systems for Career Information. (2006). *Consumer guide for evaluating career information and services.* Retrieved from http://www.acrpro.org/images/stories/uploaded_pdf/ACSCI/acsciconsumerguiderev.pdf

Coughlin, D. Shy, J. D., Sampson, J. P., Jr., & Lenz, J. G. (2010). *Distance counseling bibliography.* Retrieved from http://career.fsu.edu/documents/bibliographies/Dist_Counseling_Biblio_Aug_2010.pdf

Makela, J. P. (2009). *A case study approach to ethics in career development.* Broken Arrow, OK: National Career Development Association.

National Board for Certified Counselors, Inc., & Center for Credentialing and Education, Inc. (n. d.). *The practice of Internet counseling.* Retrieved from http://www.nbcc.org

National Career Development Association. (2007). *Code of ethics.* Retrieved from http://associationdatabase.com/aws/NCDA/asset_mana ger/get_file/3395/code_of_ethicsmay-2007.pdf

Saunders, D. E. (2007). A step-by-step approach for adopting and using distance counseling as a private practitioner. In J. F. Malone, R. M. Miller, & G. R. Walz (Eds.), *Distance counseling: Expanding the counselor's reach and impact,* 75-89. Ann Arbor, MI: Counseling Outfitters, LLC.

SUBJECT INDEX